CW00493279

# One More Hour

By the same author

*Typhoon Pilot*

# One More Hour

## Desmond Scott

## Hutchinson

**LONDON • SYDNEY • AUCKLAND • JOHANNESBURG**

This edition first published in Great Britain
in 1989 by Hutchinson,
an imprint of Century Hutchinson Ltd
Brookmount House, 62–65 Chandos Place,
Covent Garden, London WC2N 4NW

Century Hutchinson Australia (Pty) Ltd
89–91 Albion Street, Surry Hills, NSW 2010

Century Hutchinson New Zealand Limited
187 Archers Road, P O Box 40-086, Glenfield, Auckland 10

Century Hutchinson South Africa (Pty) Ltd
P O Box 337, Bergvlei 2012, South Africa

First published 1989

Printed in Hong Kong

ISBN 1 86941 045 9

# Contents

*The time shall come when thou shalt lift*
*Thine eyes the long-drawn battle in the skies to search*
*While aged peasants too amazed for words*
*Stare at the flying fleets of wondrous birds.*
*England, so long the mistress of the sea,*
*Where winds and waves confess her sovereignty,*
*Her ancient triumphs yet on high shall bear*
*And reign the sovereign of the conquered air.*

From *Luna Habitabilis*
Thomas Gray, 1737

# *Preface*

Many times I yearned for my native New Zealand. To stand again by some high country stream, as the gold of the day was deepening into purple. Such dreams were often short lived; shattered by the sound of bursting bombs or the staccato bark of ack-ack guns. The mad scramble to our aircraft and the crazy weaving climb into the heavens. Messerschmitts shining high in the sun like wicked little daggers — the hair-raising whirl of combat and the screaming breakaways that pushed your head into your chest, and your eyes into the back of your neck. Such days were common. They shattered the nerves, turned some boys into men, some into dithering idiots. It was usually the inexperienced who fell first. Most were recent graduates from the schoolroom. They silently dropped away, or blossomed earthwards into balls of orange fire.

The passing years have in no way erased the magnitude of each brief encounter, for death is a very personal thing for those who flew face to face with it. Is it any wonder even to this day, some of us avoid memorial services. Men are not supposed to cry, but when the bugle's 'Last Post' rings down the years, its long drawn out note brings back a flood of memories and the tears come with them.

# One
# The Way to the Stars

When we were members of the same class at Wigram early in 1940, Spud (Stan) Murphy and I used to fly together in big old-fashioned biplanes that went under the rather delicate name of Fairey Gordons. One day Spud would take over as pilot in the front cockpit while I would act as navigator in the rear. This cockpit was nothing more than a big draughty hole in the fuselage where you could either sit or stand on the cold metal floor. To prevent the navigator from falling or being tossed out, he wore a harness which was clipped to a metal strap that was fixed to the floor. This was commonly known as a monkey strap, presumably because it was attached to a ring on the harness in the same position as your tail should be. We had no brakes on these old crates, and when landing in a strong north-wester — which we did all too often — it was the duty of the navigator to jump down from his cockpit and hold on come hell or high water to a wing tip, to help his pilot turn the aircraft into wind. Both cockpits were quite some distance from the ground, and one day when I was pilot and Spud the navigator, he hurriedly jumped down from the aircraft, but forgot to unhitch his monkey strap. While the strong north-west wind was carrying us towards the station boundary fence, Spud was swinging by his tail — pendant fashion. The whole six feet two and 14 stone of him.

By using plenty of motor, and giving Spud a rough ride in the process, I finally managed to bring the aircraft into wind and left my cockpit to try and lift him back up the side of the fuselage so that he could unhitch himself. I was so paralytic with laughter I couldn't raise enough steam. Somehow he managed to place his size eleven boots on the top of my head and, half springing and half clawing, made his way back to the nest. The only thanks I received through the earphones as I taxied into the strong wind towards the hangar was 'Some bastards have a funny sense of humour I must say.'

No. 17 course, Wigram, mid-1940. Back row, from left: E.L. Joyce, A.C. Kelly, T.G. Webb, G.W. Alington, D.W. Gough, D. M. Walker, S.O.J. Murphy, H.G. Doherty, H.S.R. Cameron, H.G. Saunders, A.C. Mee. Front row, from left: J.T. Wallace, E.C. Ball, G.H. Grimsdale, D.S. Hamilton, J.H. Penney, R.K. Bird, D.J. Scott, R.J. Bullen, K.S. Jenner.

One evening, half a dozen of us were standing in front of No. 1 hangar watching a class member do his first solo in a Fairey Gordon. He flew the old plane in on a long steady approach and made a splendid three-pointer — only it was about 20 feet above the surface of the aerodrome. It says a lot for the old Gordon that she didn't dip a wing. As she pancaked heavily onto her two wheels and tail skid, she did the splits and her prop began cutting out great swathes of turf. Our loud guffaws could have been heard in Christchurch's city centre. Unfortunately they were heard by someone much closer. Our Flight Instructor was in the hangar office and had also witnessed Saunders' untidy landing. He didn't see things the way we did and let us know in no uncertain terms that bent axles and twisted propellers were not things to be laughed at. As he ranted and raved in his high pitched voice we found it impossible to stifle our mirth, and when one of our group farted, the situation got out of hand.

We were finally marched off to our barrack block and instructed to remain there until further notice. The rafters in the old wooden hut rang with our laughter and when Saunders came in about an hour later, looking like a Saint Bernard dog that had just been scolded, we almost brought the roof down.

The bent Gordon was carted into the repair and maintenance section, its axle removed, straightened and delivered to our Flight room, where we spent a number of unhappy evenings trying to put a polish on it.

This measure of punitive detention only reinforced my instinct to steer clear of the officer class. Recently commissioned, most had transformed themselves into sarcastic martinets, and while exercising their new found authority, would leave us pilot trainees moping about Wigram like sick storks. Laughter is a necessary tonic for all wartime flyers, yet seldom — if ever — did I see an instructor smile. I learned early in my career to keep well clear of the pipe-smoking officer too. This unhappy-looking breed would peer at you through half-closed eyes and a haze of smoke. You could almost see their minds revolving like well-oiled grindstones. Most were too slow to make mistakes and we pupils were usually able to remove ourselves by the time they saw the light.

Seven weeks after Saunders pranged the Fairey Gordon, our class said goodbye to Wigram and sailed away to the other side of the world. France had already fallen to the might of Hitler's Panzers but we gave little thought to that. Each day, like those of our schoolboy summers, was a new

Standing in front of a Fairey Gordon, Wigram, May 1940. Left to right: E.L. ('Nipper') Joyce (shot down and killed, Evreux); R.J. Bullen (killed off Le Touquet); J.T. Wallace (killed off Orfordness); S.O.J. Murphy (P.O.W.); D.J. Scott; J.H. Penney (Staff pilot); D.M. Walker (killed in Scotland); H.S.R. Cameron (Staff pilot).

adventure. The wide blue Pacific. The strange sights and smells of the tropics. Panama City. The West Indies. The thousand and one pleasures of sailing towards new horizons. In fact it wasn't until we were chased back into Bermuda by the pocket battleship *Admiral Scheer* that our minds became focused on the war in Europe.

The transition between peace and war became very real and very earnest. We were to learn that the *Admiral Scheer* had sunk ten of our convoy including the armed merchant cruiser *Jervis Bay,* whose epic struggle against such superior odds will live forever in the annals of all who follow the sea. After a few days in Bermuda we sped off on our own to Halifax, Nova Scotia, where we joined another convoy bound for the United Kingdom.

The first half of the crossing was uneventful, due I think to a terrific storm that raged for most of the time. The second half of the crossing was quite a different story. As the seas quietened, the presence of the enemy was the source of a permanent fear. The days were not so bad — apart from the sighting of a lone Focke Wulf Condor which shadowed our convoy for an hour or two on a very calm Sunday. The wail of

The author (shirtless) with other aircrew members aboard the Mataroa on the way to England, 1940.

The Mataroa off Bermuda.

the ship's siren calling us to boat stations sent a shiver down the spine. With sickly grins we did our best to appear unperturbed, but it was the ever-clowning Mun Walker who helped to ease our fears. He arrived on deck with an enamel chamber-pot on his head. If the days appeared to be a slow drag toward our destination the nights were the very opposite.

The crunch, crunch, crunch of the depth charges. They

Boat drill.

shook the ship and shook us too. At this time we were neither sailors nor airmen, and could only lie in our dark cabins and with wide eyes hope for the dawn. Sometimes we would make our way on deck where great fires could be seen to the rear of our convoy. Tankers that had been torpedoed and left to the mercy of the seas. So bright were the conflagrations that the whole convoy would stand out in bold relief. Such sights were common. They made the heart beat faster and reminded us that we were now boys in a man's world — and that world was far from home.

We eventually arrived off the coast of Scotland, and after sailing up the Clyde, said goodbye to our ship and boarded the train that was to take us from Glasgow to London. The Empire's capital was the end of a long journey but any ideas of thankfulness were soon dispelled. Someone had lifted my suitcase from the luggage van, and I entered my RAF service at Uxbridge lacking most of my feathers.

Uxbridge, in the London suburb of Stanmore, was the receiving station for most overseas aircrew. It was not a flying station, just a huge reception centre which in pre-war days acted as a ground training school for those recruits who had entered the permanent RAF. Due to a grave shortage of aircrew our stay there was all too short, although it did give us enough time to pay several visits to the heart of the great metropolis. The so-called Battle of Britain — according to the scribes — had just been won, yet the night skies and parts of London itself often resembled scattered portraits of Dante's *Inferno*. The Luftwaffe was obviously far from finished, and the only difference between the day and night battles was that at night, other than the odd bomber that was illuminated by searchlights, the enemy couldn't be seen, and continued to spread his warload upon a shocked and defiant London. It was a dangerous place. Noisy, frightening, and at times even comical.

One night Mun Walker and I were leaving a Forces' dance at the Overseas League to meet up with some of our fellow pilots at the New Zealand Forces' Club in Charing Cross Road. It was only a short distance and we agreed to walk, but as we stepped out into the blackout a taxi pulled up at the door and let two people out. As they left the cab Mun and I hopped in and the driver slammed the door shut and took off post haste. There was a particularly heavy raid on at the time and after rattling up the Strand for what seemed too long a time, I got the impression the driver had forgotten his passengers and was heading fast for the suburbs. I asked Mun if he had given the driver the right directions. His reply was that he hadn't spoken to him and that he thought I had given the order. I wasted no time in opening up the glass partition that separated the passenger compartment from the driver and slapped him on the shoulder. His reaction was immediate. He jammed on the brakes which nearly hurled me through the windscreen. He didn't say a word for a full ten seconds then with a face I could see in the blackout, blurted out 'Cor blimey mate, I didn't know you were there.'

He wouldn't take us back to the Strand so we spent the night in a police station. Quite a profitable night too, for the members of the constabulary were not the best of poker players. We arrived back at Uxbridge next morning smoking cigars in the back seat of a Rolls Royce. The car had been requisitioned by the State, but I believe the cigars had once been the property of a bombed-out tobacconist.

Besides being an aircrew reception centre, Uxbridge was also the home of the aircrew 'Devil's Lottery', for it was from Uxbridge that we learned the role each of us would play in the air war over Europe. Bomber, Fighter, or Coastal. I say 'Devil's Lottery' because each posting to an operational command bore the same measure of chance. We had already been told by members of the RAF that a posting to a night bomber squadron was the equivalent of a one-way ticket to the grave — to Blenheim day bombers, a similar fate — but with a journey through hell on the way. Fighter Command was every pilot's idea of heaven, for in the realms of the high-flyer there was ample scope to exercise any natural flair although, as we were later to learn, nine times out of ten contact with the enemy was brief and our fortunes undecided. One moment the sky was a mad whirl of aircraft, the next it was empty.

As the war progressed and the Luftwaffe turned its back on Britain to take on the might of the Russians, the RAF had to re-shape its ideas, with the result that a new breed of aircraft appeared — the fighter bomber, the poor relation of Fighter Command. Bombs were slung under the wings of

Hurricanes, which became known as Hurribombers. Spitfires would shepherd these versatile little aircraft in low level attacks against enemy shipping and airfields, operations that were both hair-raising and spectacular and also bloody dangerous.

As with Bomber and Coastal Command, this unglamorous role was always subordinated to the deeds of the high-flying fighter, yet some of us were soon to learn that it was far more dangerous trying to destroy enemy aircraft on the ground than attempting to shoot them out of the sky. In the German defence system, light flak was always present and from a low-attack pilot's point of view it was the most lethal weapon ever invented. Thus the Jabo or fighter bomber so feared by the enemy was quickly forgotten. It even came to pass that the brave image of Bomber Command became tarnished by the acrid ashes of Hamburg and Dresden. Few wanted to know that twice as many Allied airmen were shot down in a single night over Nuremberg as were lost in the entire Battle of Britain. So it was only natural that we all wanted to be fighter pilots. To strut around with our tunic top button undone to reveal to all and sundry that we were in fact members of Churchill's Few.

Thus it came as a rude shock for some when they learned they were being posted into Bomber Command. Mun Walker was one such posting and he had my sympathy as we bade each other farewell in a boyish tearful way. He was posted to Wellingtons based at Lossiemouth in northern Scotland, and was killed in an air crash within a few days of his arrival.

# Two
# Sutton Bridge

'Spud' Murphy, 'Nipper' Joyce, Dick 'Armchair' Bullen, Kelly and I were posted to Fighter Command to fly Hurricanes. Since none of us had flown anything more complicated than slow old biplanes it was necessary for us to attend an operational training unit where we were to complete a conversion course and also learn the rudiments if not the more advanced skills of modern air war.

We were packed off from Uxbridge like a bunch of schoolboys, each with a rail warrant that would take us to RAF Station Sutton Bridge, a grass airfield and hutted camp a few miles west of Kings Lynn and bordered to the east by the Wash. It was to prove one of the most uninteresting parts of England I was ever to serve in. Not only was the surrounding countryside cold, low and wet, but the station's domestic complex was built to match. A series of wooden huts that resembled aircraft crates all camouflaged in black and green and designed to sleep about 20 pilots to each hut — ten a side. This accommodation was both ridiculous and austere. Our beds were iron stretchers that concertinaed into a third of their length when not in use. On each bed were three square canvas-covered squabs filled with sawdust. Placed end to end they took the place of the more orthodox mattress, but since we were not issued with sheets it was virtually impossible to keep them in line or in fact together. This brainchild of some stupid inventor may have suited desert conditions but was hardly compatible with the conditions that normally made up a Lincolnshire winter. We usually woke up with our backsides filling a gap between the squabs and resting on the cold iron slats that took the place of the more conventional springs. This discomfort was partly overcome by placing thick layers of newspaper beneath the squabs and sleeping in our overcoats. Nonetheless most survivors of the Sutton Bridge days will always remember those airforce beds. Their inventor should have taken his place alongside Hermann Göring and his cohorts at the Nuremberg trials. This may sound severe but as we progressed through our various degrees of operational training the accident rate became appalling and I have often wondered how many young lives were lost through lack of sleep.

Our time at Sutton Bridge represented what later in the war we would have described as a pressure-cooker course. The Battle of Britain had deprived the squadrons of Fighter Command of many pilots and replacements were required urgently to replenish their ranks.

Before being allowed to fly the Hurricane we first of all had to go through a brief period of dual instruction on Miles Masters — a delightful little monoplane powered by a Rolls Royce Kestrel engine. Even this was a very long stride from our biplane days at Wigram. After two or three circuits and landings my Battle of Britain pilot instructor climbed out of his cockpit and with a slap on my back said 'She's all yours'. I was so surprised I became a little confused and nearly turned around and took off down wind. After a week on Masters and the noisy little American Harvard I was told by my instructor he considered I was sufficiently advanced in my tuition to take to the skies in a Hurricane. The morning I was detailed to fulfil my dreams started with a disaster. A Hampden twin-engined bomber crashed in a field about a mile from our dispersal hut. It had apparently been engaged in fighter affiliation practice with some Spitfires from a neighbouring station. One of the Spitfire pilots had misjudged his distance and collided with the target aircraft, almost severing its tail section. The Hampden when crashing had burst into flames. Several of us scrambled into a car and set off at high speed towards the huge column of black smoke in the hope of giving some assistance to its crew. Unfortunately by the time we reached the burning aircraft all except one had been consumed by the flames. He was lying to one side of the burning wreckage, his uniform still smouldering and his legs at right angles to his body. We dragged him away from the flaming wreckage and propped him against a tree. He had lost his eyelids and his sightless eyes looked like white marbles set deep in his blackened and swollen face. An ambulance was soon on the scene and we helped to lift him onto a stretcher. He was quietly sobbing and as the ambulance drove away I could hear him calling for his mother.

The Hurricane I was to fly became unserviceable and it was not until the afternoon that it was repaired and I could lower myself into its cockpit. Flight Lieutenant Sing climbed onto the port wing and gave me my final instructions — brief and very much to the point. 'Good luck Scott. She's all yours. Break it and I'll break your ruddy fingers.'

Such was my introduction to one of the nicest and most versatile aircraft I ever had the pleasure to fly. As I pushed the throttle lever forward the Rolls Royce Merlin surged into life and I felt a heavy pressure on my back as we accelerated across the airfield and rocketed into the air in the direction of Wisbech. Quickly climbing to 15 000 feet I could see many places below that were familiar to me from my maps. The wide expanse of the Wash. Spalding, Peterborough, Kings Lynn and Downham Market. This was England and I was above it in a Hurricane! How quickly the world had changed. In my youth I counted my years by the summers. Those long lazy barefooted days along the river, where we would fish or swim, or lie baking in the sun telling tall stories about the girls who shared our class. We shed those years for long trousers, short haircuts and furtive cigarettes. To be swept away in a war was a new adventure, which lifted our egos and added a new dimension to our years. My training days at Wigram were far behind me as I flew out to sea high above the Wash.

We started our airborne partnership with a couple of loops followed by a series of slow rolls. She proved to be a most delightful companion and even more amenable than Sing had led me to believe. When my half hour was up I let down the undercarriage, put on a few degrees of flap and began a wide circuit of the aerodrome. As I came in on my final approach I could see the still smouldering wreck of the Hampden, and made a rather bumpy landing — due, I think, to trying to be too careful.

As our training progressed, a number of pilots fell by the wayside and were transferred to other Commands. Some I felt sorry for. You could see at a glance that they would even be uncomfortable in a saddle and were obviously not cut out to be fighter pilots. They were simply victims of their earlier *ab initio* training days. Some chairborne officer with more seniority than sense — and there were plenty around in our training days — had drafted his subordinates like sheep through a gate. Thus the slow splay-footed boy with the dull eyes and ample paunch had to compete with the athlete in a race that was both dangerous and fast. One glaring example of poor selection was an Australian who must have stood six foot six inches in his bare feet. He couldn't fit into the closed cockpit of a Hurricane without a perpetual stoop. One afternoon he came into land with his canopy closed and I was not surprised to see his Hurricane hit the ground with some force before frog-leaping across the aerodrome and finishing up on its nose — its tail sticking up straight like a totem pole. He was posted on to Wellingtons which had much more head room and spent a brief period in Bomber Command before meeting his end in the night sky above Stuttgart.

Another boy from our flight couldn't stand the strain and suffered a mental breakdown. A quiet, rather effeminate sergeant from Nottingham, he lost his best friend — and right in front of our eyes. The friend had capsized his Hurricane when coming in to land and although the aircraft was slow in catching fire, its pilot was unable to get himself clear of his cockpit. His piercing screams rent the air and scared the daylights out of us, but since the aircraft was too heavy to lift by hand, we could only stand by helplessly and await the arrival of the firetender and mobile crane. In spite of the sterling work of both vehicles' crews it was too late by the time they recovered the pilot. Next morning the young sergeant was arrested while trying to bite into the wing of a Hurricane and was later committed to a mental asylum.

Spud, Nipper, Bullen, Kelly and I made the grade and were posted from Sutton Bridge to our operational squadrons. Spud and Kelly were posted into Ten Group where both came to grief in most unfortunate ways. Spud was shot down while attacking ground targets on the Brest Peninsula and spent over four years as a prisoner of war. Kelly went down into the sea and would have probably survived had we worn dinghys as well as Mae Wests at that time. Instead, he was faced with a long swim, for the Air Sea

20

Rescue Service failed to find him, and although he eventually made the shore, he died soon after the Coast Guards picked him up.

Bullen was posted into the newly formed 485 Squadron, but his time in it was all too short. He was shot down by a 109 off Le Touqet — the first member of this New Zealand squadron to lose his life in action.

Nipper Joyce and I were posted into No. 3 Squadron. It had taken a severe hammering in France and the Battle of Britain and was recuperating at Skeabrae, an airfield under construction near Scapa Flow in the Orkney Islands. It was January 1941. Thus began five years of my life as a pilot in the wartime RAF. An age when the excitement, the fear and dread, the sheer swift clamour of it all burned into the memory, so that much of life since has been a slow-moving backwater by comparison.

# Three
# A Point of No Return

After completing our course at Sutton Bridge, we were given seven days' leave before proceeding to our squadrons. Our earlier brief visits to London during our stay at Uxbridge had whetted our appetites for the metropolis. The Londoners were most receptive to Dominion airmen and many friendships had already been established, so it was only natural that without exception we all made a return visit to this great city.

In my earlier visit I had become friendly with a young WREN officer whom I had met at the Overseas League. Phillipa was a most attractive girl, although she would bombard me with letters which I never seemed to have the time or the inclination to answer. She was also most anxious for me to meet her parents — an event that promised little comfort for me, but one I knew I had to face if I wished to retain their daughter's friendship. Ultimately I accepted an invitation to dine with the family at their Kensington home, and arrived sharp on the dot of seven as suggested.

I was met at the entrance by Phillipa, her mother and father, two affable aunts, and the son of the house, Master Frederick — aged about eight. One of the aunts had at some time visited the Antipodes and while she was doing her best to impress me with her knowledge of 'Syderney' over a pre-dinner sherry, young Frederick was looking at me wide-eyed, as if I had just fallen off the moon. I sensed trouble ahead and had I been in my more familiar place in the cockpit, would have turned my gun button from 'safe' to the 'fire' position.

After our sherry, we were led into the dining room by an elderly housemaid-cook whose wrinkled face, Roman nose and flat lace cap reminded me of a Border Leicester sheep. When entering, the first thing I noticed was a beautiful stairway which in its reach for the next floor almost circled the room. Phillipa's parents sat at opposite ends of the rectangular table while I was seated between Phillipa and the much travelled aunt. Young Fred and the other aunt shared the opposite side. I can't recall the flavour of the soup, but I do remember that the roast beef which followed was exceptionally rare in the true English tradition. I always preferred my meat well done. By the time I was half way through the second course, the history of the British Navy and the Sydney Harbour Bridge, I was seized with a sudden desire to sneeze. Hurriedly putting down my knife and fork I whipped out a handkerchief and though quick enough to partly stifle it I couldn't contain both ends at the one time, and my muffled sneeze was punctuated by a sharp report. I had hardly whispered pardon, when young Fred, who had been very quiet, suddenly came to life. I dared not look at the laughing little critter and could have buried my head in the Brussels sprouts, but it was his father who accepted the challenge on my behalf.

'Now Frederick, if you don't pull yourself together up you go to the bathroom.'

Young Fred may have tried hard, but it wasn't good enough and after a brief period of silence followed by loud peals of boyish laughter, he was sent sniggering up the stairs. The bathroom was on the upper landing almost directly above my head, so he might just as well have stayed in his place at the table, for every few minutes our small talk was almost drowned out from above.

I think Fred's father was enjoying my predicament for he neglected to save me from further embarrassment. Our dessert comprised stewed apples and custard, and being a true-blue New Zealander and thus a product of our Plunket system I looked around for the cream. In my befuddled state I had forgotten that in wartime England, cream was almost a thing of the past. Two small jugs of similar pattern stood before me in the candlelight. I picked up the nearest and remember thinking as I poured a little over my pudding — 'This cream is of the tinned variety — probably Nestles'. The first spoonful made my hair bristle and I felt as if someone had shot an arrow into the back of my neck. A few more mouthfuls and I had to give up in favour of a large glass of water.

At the conclusion of the meal the womenfolk departed for another room leaving the master of the house to take care of me and the port. After I had put one of his proffered cigars into my mouth he leant over to light it and with a wry smile, said in a half whisper — 'How did the apple and custard go with the horseradish sauce?'

When leaving I had some difficulty in saying goodbye. I almost had to promise, like General MacArthur, that I would return, and soon, to their house in Kensington Gardens.

The exigency of war can be a legitimate excuse for many things, but I already knew it would take more than a team of wild horses to drag me back to that address.


When our leave had expired, Nipper Joyce and I boarded a train for Aberdeen, where we were to link up with a ferry boat bound for the Orkney Islands. It proved to be a cold miserable journey, for it snowed so hard it brought our train to a halt somewhere between Dundee and Aberdeen.

Fortunately it was near a golf course, and after disembarking we trudged through deep snow to the golf club buildings where we spent the night on the hard cold floor as guests of the Salvation Army. It was a most uncomfortable night, but I shall never forget that cheerful little band of helpers. Even after all these years, the sight of a Salvation Army uniform and its quaint little bonnet sends my thoughts racing back to those dark dangerous days of the forties.

We eventually arrived in Aberdeen, a city my mother used to describe to me as being built of gleaming white granite. She had left Scotland for New Zealand at the age of sixteen and I couldn't help thinking that her last look at this coastal city had been taken through rose-coloured glasses. The sun had not yet risen and everything looked dull and dingy. What is more, after spending a sleepless night on the train, I was both hungry and longing for a hot bath.

We entered a hotel and asked the receptionist if she would kindly allow us the use of a bathroom. She agreed wholeheartedly but said it would cost us ten shillings each. Since a sergeant pilot's pay was only twelve and sixpence a day, this sounded rather excessive and we told her so.

Besides, our time in London had taken care of most of our change, and what little we had left was needed for the rest of our journey to the Orkneys. Nipper, though short in stature, was highly vocal, and told the elderly receptionist what she could do with her bath. The redhead behind the desk responded with her own verbal abuse, but so rapidly and in such a broad Scottish accent that most of it escaped my hearing. However, we got the message, left the pub and set forth up the main street.

Nipper was still giving me a running commentary on what he thought of the Scots, when a well dressed elderly gentleman stopped us as we were about to enter another hotel. He pointed to our New Zealand shoulder flashes and informed us that he was a former merchant marine officer and had had many happy visits to New Zealand while employed by the Shaw Savill Shipping Company. Nipper wasted little time in telling him about our brush with the hotel receptionist. This amused our new-found friend immensely, for he roared with laughter, and turning us both around, led us to his own home where we bathed and shaved before sitting down to a delicious breakfast of porridge and kippers. Our host and his plump little wife were a charming couple and did much to restore my childhood dreams of Scotland's granite city.

We boarded our ferry boat and set sail for the Orkneys as night was falling — presumably to remain out of sight of the German bomber crews who made a habit of attacking our coastal shipping off the north-east coast of Scotland, particularly in the region of Peterhead.

Like our train trip, it was another traumatic journey. The ship was crowded with sailors and soldiers, and seating accommodation seemed non-existent. I partly solved the latter problem by enthroning myself on a lavatory — not the quietest of places, but at least it took most of the weight off my legs. Had the sea remained calm, I would have spent the night there, but unfortunately around about midnight it cut up rough. The two lavatories on either side of me became rather busy places, and the noise of swinging doors and the smell of passengers retching forced me to vacate my hollow chair and remove myself to another part of the ship.

I was so exhausted by the time we reached our destination,

B Flight, No. 3 Squadron, Orkney Islands January 1941. All killed except J. Shaw (third from left). 'Nipper' Joyce squats in front.

I still can't remember where we disembarked at Scapa Flow — Lyness or Kirkwall. All I remember is that it was bitterly cold and snow lay everywhere.

Skeabrae was one hell of a place. The two asphalt runways were a luxury for our Hurricanes, but everything else was either half finished or surrounded by a sea of mud and slush. Gale force winds would sweep down from the North Sea almost every day, driving snow into deep drifts and filling the ditches that had been excavated in preparation for the laying of pipes for the station's drainage system. I have good reason to remember the latter.

One night two of us fell into one and had a hard time finding a way out. We had set out to rob the bunker of a steam traction-engine in order to help with our coal supply. While Johnnie Shaw was up on the bunker he knocked down a large lump of coal which fell on my left foot. I let out a bellow that must have startled even the engine and limped off over the crusty snow in what I thought was a short-cut to our hut. The snow-filled ditch must have been close to six feet deep and I only managed to get out by walking on Johnnie's shoulders and then pulling him out. We made our

26

Castletown, North Scotland. The guns are made of wood, and footmarks are to fox the Hun.

sleeping quarters without being challenged although it must have been a fairly close shave, for a few minutes later we could hear a noisy argument coming from the hut next door.

There were no trees on the Orkneys and most of the civilians who were working on the station's complex were from Ireland. The war didn't seem to mean a thing to them, and it was not uncommon to see a bunch of them huddled around a coal-fired brazier playing cards. The defence forces guarding the islands were the very opposite. If they couldn't find any Huns to shoot at they gave *us* their full attention. The Navy at Scapa Flow was the worst offender — their motto being to shoot first and ask questions afterwards. We were not sorry when the squadron was ordered back to the mainland — even if just across the water to Castletown, near Thurso at the very northern tip of Scotland. This too was an aerodrome still under construction.

Castletown's domestic complex was almost non-existent, the squadron's sergeant pilots being housed in rough wooden huts similar to the ones we had at Sutton Bridge — they were also quite some distance from the sergeants' mess. Near our billets were several long-barrelled wooden guns set in peat block surrounds. To make these guns appear authentic to the Luftwaffe air reconnaissance we were ordered every day or two to walk across the snow-covered area between our billets and the guns, so that our footprints in the snow might prove a deterrent to our opponents. The Luftwaffe kept well clear of us during our stay at Castletown, so our frozen footsteps may not have been entirely wasted.

The squadron's dispersal accommodation was quite unique too. It consisted of a small house requisitioned from a local crofter, a dismal stone building set on a slight rise allowing its occupants to look out over the aerodrome towards Dunnet Bay.

The airfield had two long concrete runways criss-crossed on what appeared to be a sea of mud. Most of this was covered in wind-blown snow and large patches of water. Any aircraft that happened to stray off the runway or perimeter tracks sank like a crab onto its belly or turned turtle onto its back with even more disastrous results.

One afternoon while two of us were strapped into our cockpits on instant readiness, a lone Hurricane came screaming down out of the blue and buried itself nose first in the mud. It was only about 50 yards in front of us. We both leapt out of our cockpits and rushed over to the stricken aircraft. The pilot, who wore a Norwegian uniform, was killed instantly. Several other B-Flight pilots arrived on the scene and we lifted his remains out of the cockpit and carried him onto the tarmac taxiway. His uniform looked like a bag full of blood and bones — many of the latter having pierced his trouser legs.

After the dead pilot had been taken away by ambulance, Sgt Todd and I received a severe reprimand from our Flight Commander for leaving our cockpits without permission!

The cold of Castletown and the long winter nights did little to cheer us up or bind us together as a squadron. We had two Polish pilots in B-Flight. Both had escaped to England after the collapse of Poland and had been readily accepted by the RAF. Sgt Beale had been an officer and product of Poland's Military Staff College. The other, Sgt Gallico, had been a non-commissioned officer in the Polish Air Force. Apparently there was a very wide gap in their social status, for the ex-officer Beale treated his countryman like a serf. Much to our surprise, Gallico did as he was told and spent a miserable time as his master's batman. He was made to clean Beale's tunic buttons, polish his shoes and flying boots, and wait on him with his shaving gear. This treatment by one sergeant pilot of another annoyed me and I asked Sgt Beale if he would kindly leave Gallico alone. We were outside our hut at the time, on snow that would have been about eight or nine inches deep and supporting a fairly heavy crust. Beale lost his temper and came strutting towards me, hands on hips and looking like a Polish Mussolini. He told me to mind my own 'pluddy binez'. Our argument was resolved in a matter of seconds. I sat him on his backside before turning him over and pushing his face into the snow. Thereafter Gallico was able to take his place among his fellow sergeant pilots on an equal footing. How long this arrangement lasted I don't really know, for about a week later both were posted down south to Polish squadrons operating in the Northolt Wing. I sincerely hope they weren't posted to the same squadron since, as I found out later, Polish squadrons in the RAF had a habit of setting their own code of rules. I didn't see either again but I often think of Gallico, as he was by far the better pilot of the two.

A few days after the Poles had left, our squadron received its own posting notice. With whoops of delight we learned that we were to move south to Martlesham Heath near Ipswich on the northern flank of No. 11 Group, Fighter Command's premier Group covering the London area and most of the south coast. We were to take our place alongside such famous stations as Manston, Tangmere, Hawkinge, Kenley, Biggin Hill, Hornchurch and North Weald — stations that had borne the brunt of the Luftwaffe's assault against England. It was like being ordered into the firing line, only in this case, by the time we arrived, the enemy had largely flown. Consequently our activities were confined to mundane convoy patrols over the Thames estuary and the straits of Dover. I saw no sign of the enemy during any of these patrols, although I was nearly shot down by one of our own destroyers. However, it was all good training and I believe most of the squadron's pilots who were not killed in accidents benefited from these long hours of relative boredom, and in so doing helped to prepare themselves for the more arduous and perilous days and nights that were yet to come.

# Four
# Reap the Wild Winds

We hadn't been long at Martlesham Heath when we were
joined by No. 71 Squadron. All its pilots were American and
it was known as the First 'Eagle' Squadron. Unlike normal
RAF squadrons, all its pilots were commissioned, and since
America was not at that time involved in the war, they were
only permitted to fly on defensive sorties. As we were not
politicians, this did not concern us. However, the fact that all
wore the King's Commission, did. Most aircrew in the RAF
were sergeant pilots — a non-commissioned aircrew rank,
which I could never reconcile myself to accept. The pilot of
an aircraft was always its captain, and it was not uncommon
— particularly in Bomber and Coastal Commands — for a
sergeant pilot to have a team of officers as his crew. His word
was law when in the air, but when back on the ground the
roles were reversed. He might then have to refer to his
commissioned rear gunner as 'Sir'! I always believed, and

Re-arming a Hurricane IIc, Essex.

still do, that if a man could fly an expensive aircraft on dangerous operations, and in most cases be responsible for a crew of six or more while doing so, he was well qualified to hold the King's Commission. In No. 3 Squadron it was the sergeant pilots who showed the greatest degree of initiative, and I considered on the whole they were better pilots than the officers we had in the Squadron at that time.

Chesley Petersen's boys in No. 71 Squadron were a great bunch and carried out their restricted duties with enthusiasm and self-confidence. They took a great deal of the weight off our shoulders, for at that time No. 3 Squadron was reduced to twelve pilots when our strength should have been at least twenty. Furthermore we were committed to a dual role — both day- and night-fighting. Within a day or two of our arrival at Martlesham Heath our numbers were almost reduced to eleven. My goggles had blown off while we were taking off on a scramble. This didn't concern me at the time, for once airborne and with your canopy shut you were better off without them, except when on attack, particularly if it involved shipping. They helped to prevent any glass splinters from being blasted into your eyes. Mine had blown off just as I was about to become airborne and that evening I walked out to the centre of the aerodrome to retrieve them. I had some trouble finding them, and just as I bent down to pick them up two Heinkels bombers came in low over the northern boundary and dropped their bombs in our dispersal area. Fortunately we had just been released from cockpit readiness, for my own Hurricane received a near miss and was blown to smithereens. As the enemy swept in low over the aerodrome, one of their rear gunners had spotted me out in the middle of the airfield and gave me his full attention. At school I had held the record over a hundred yards, but I think I carved several seconds off my time as bits of turf spattered onto the backs of my legs. He was either a poor shot or was laughing so much at my predicament he couldn't aim straight. While sprinting for the outfield I dropped my goggles again. They could be there still, for I never found the courage nor the inclination to have another look.

The reason for our shift south soon became obvious. Instead of waiting for the Luftwaffe to visit Britain, the hierarchy of the RAF had decided to take the air war into the enemy's domain. Not only were we expected to carry out attacks against enemy shipping and targets in Belgium and France, we were also expected to do night fighter patrols over London — a dual role that was versatile but very exhausting. We could cover most operations from Martlesham Heath, but fighter nights over London had to be carried out from Debden on account of its runways and better night-flying facilities. Thus we could be attacking shipping in the morning, escorting Blenheim or Stirling bombers over France in the afternoon and flying defensive patrols over London on the same night.

Attacks on enemy shipping, which came under the code name of 'Roadstead' operations, became more frequent as spring blossomed into summer. Enemy ships which were trying to run the gauntlet through the English Channel were always well protected by flak ships. These operations were generally arranged at short notice for it was normally through pure luck that our targets were sighted anyway. Enemy ships had a habit of making their way along the coast of France by steaming close to the shore and in and out of the many ports along their course. If we could catch them between ports well and good, but we still had to be quick. Consequently most 'Roadstead' operations that were laid on

The author on the wing of a Hurricane IIc, Martlesham Heath, May 1941.

at short notice never ran according to our briefings, and most finished up in chaos.

One afternoon a large merchantman was seen by one of the reconnaissance pilots of 501 Squadron who were operating out of Hawkinge. By the time we were briefed it was anticipated she would be half way between Le Touquet and Boulogne. Our briefing was short and simple. We would escort three Blenheim light bombers at nought feet and on approaching the target the Hurricanes would draw ahead and rake the flak ships with machine-gun and cannon fire. At this time we were being re-equipped with Hurricane Mark IIc's. These were fitted with four 20 mm Hispano cannons, but most of our squadron aircraft had either twelve Brownings, or the original number of eight. As we approached the convoy the flak came flying up thick and fast and two of the Blenheims were shot down and crashed into the sea. I finished my ammunition on the flak ship I had selected and went to join up with the surviving Blenheim, but it too hit the sea, and we arrived back over the cliffs of Dover minus two Hurricanes of 242 Squadron who had shared our task. Hurricanes were scattered over a wide area, and all flat out for home base. The operations controller ordered us to land at Manston where we hurriedly re-armed and refuelled and set off again to the target with three Beaufort torpedo bombers that had arrived up from Ford. This next attack was almost a repetition of the first. Two of the Beauforts were shot down by flak on their run in to the target and the third crash-landed without engaging the enemy. In our first attack on this convoy I was thankful that there were no enemy fighters over the scene of action. In the second attack they were waiting for us.

After completing my two attacks on a flak ship I pulled up to join a gaggle of aircraft I thought to be the rest of the squadron. On closer inspection I almost choked. They were all ME-109s and ready for business, their black crosses almost blinding me. As they turned towards me I shot underneath them and hugging the sea, went full bore for Dover. Contrary to what I had been told, the 109 had much longer legs than a Hurricane, for not only were they shooting at me from behind, they would also fly ahead and attack me on the beam. While training at Sutton Bridge my instructor, Flt Lt

Sing, had'told me to skid my aircraft when attacked from the rear. I am sure that brief word of advice saved my life, for as soon as I saw tracer firing at me from the rear I hammered my foot onto the left rudder bar. I heard a few shots hit my aircraft but most sped past to starboard. Two or three 109s chased me all the way back to Dover but as soon as I pulled up over the cliffs they turned away towards France. I found the Squadron already back at Manston. Instead of doing two attacks on the flak ships as briefed they had only done the one. I had some heated words with my flight commander who had lead the Squadron and I think it was only his conscience that saved me from being matted for insubordination. I should have kept my peace for he was killed next morning when colliding with another Hurricane during a simple exercise in the skies above Hertfordshire.

Escorting day bombers over France at this stage of the war was a bloody and useless waste of time. Admittedly Russia was now involved in the war, and it was the duty of Britain to tie up as much of the Luftwaffe as possible. But the returns for such operations were out of all proportion to our losses. With Malta fighting for her very existence and short of modern fighter aircraft it seemed extraordinary that Spitfires by the hundreds should be retained in England to carry out trifling little raids against Hitler's Europe.

One typical operation was carried out in the afternoon of 19 July. We were to escort three of the new Stirling four-engined bombers to a power station at Lille. No. 3 Squadron was to act as close escort, with a reminder that we had to keep in close to the bombers and should on no account leave them to engage enemy aircraft. That duty was left to the many squadrons of Spitfires that acted as escort and high cover. In other words our Hurricanes were accompanying the bombers in tight formation to assist the morale of the bomber crews. We were flying at about 15000 feet, the escort cover about 3 000 feet above us, and the top cover sending off vapour trails near the stratosphere. Spitfires galore. The target was obscured by cloud and the bombers turned for home. When in the vicinity of St. Omer I caught sight of two yellow-nosed 109s to the rear of the

No. 3 Squadron crest.

escort cover and at the same height. They were also seen by the Hornchurch Wing Leader who was leading the squadrons in the escort cover. His warning was both loud and high-pitched, but instead of being set upon by one of his squadrons, the two lone enemy aircraft zoomed down from above and poured long bursts of tracer into the very Stirling I was tucked alongside. One of its starboard motors burst into flames, and when the enemy fighter crossed underneath me while diving away I could see right into his cockpit. So confident was the pilot I could almost picture him polishing his fingernails.

The stricken Stirling jettisoned its bombs and four of the crew baled out — one from somewhere up front, for he rolled head over heels along the side of the fuselage before his chute opened after he passed over the tail.

Had I chased after the enemy fighter I would have been on my own and no doubt court-martialled for neglecting my duty — providing I had been fortunate enough to make base.

If our Squadron was detailed for night employment over London we would fly into Debden after the last operation of the day. Debden was much closer to London and our underground dispersal quiet, comfortable and a place to sleep if circumstances permitted.

Fighter nights over London were referred to as 'forward layers'. The London flak barrage was restricted to a certain height. Above that and at every 500 feet would be a Hurricane. The top layer was at 23000 feet and each Hurricane pilot had to stick rigidly to his allotted height. We drew our height bands from a hat and I always seemed to have the misfortune to draw one of the higher levels. It was hard enough finding a Hun at his bombing height, which was normally between 10000 and 15000 feet, but to find one at 23000 feet was reaching for the impossible. 10 May 1941 was a typical example. I drew the top layer. It was the night Hess baled out over Scotland and was probably the heaviest night raid London ever experienced. The entire city seemed to be on fire, yet the only Hun I saw was on fire at about 6000 feet. Some lucky Hurricane pilot had collared it when making his way down to his home base. Such was the luck of the draw. Bob English, one of our own sergeant pilots and a good friend, was not so lucky. He was a minute late reporting to dispersal and, as a punitive measure, was put in charge of the runway chance light. An ME-110 came in low, strafed the traffic control vehicle and put a high explosive cannon shell through Bob while doing so.

# Chapter Five
# The Heavenly Arena

Mid-summer of 1941 produced a marked change in our fortunes. We began to reap the benefits of Canada's Empire air training scheme. Pilots began arriving in at such a rate we soon had a surplus. Some, including one or two of our more experienced pilots, were posted away. Nipper Joyce was sent out to the Middle East where he shot down 11 enemy aircraft as a member of 73 Squadron. An outstanding little pilot, he finally came to grief over Evreux on 18 June 1944 while flying a Mustang of 122 Squadron.

As our activities increased, so too did our losses — and our accident rate. I could never understand the latter, for if any aircraft was free of vices it was the Hurricane. We lost pilots through spinning into the ground, colliding in mid-air or simply disappearing. One such pilot was Dick Bruin. I cover his ending in some detail as he was so typical of our squadron life at that time. Dick was from Manchester. Six feet tall, large grey eyes and ears that stuck out like a pair of ping-pong bats. He arrived in at A-Flight dispersal after spending the best part of two days on a train. This hadn't improved his looks, nor had it helped to tidy up his uniform. In fact the CO said he looked as rough as a badger's arse and that he would be happy if Dick rejoined the squadron after a hot bath. Dick was to share my billet in a brick bungalow just over the boundary fence from Martlesham Heath. I had shared this room with a number of pilots before Dick arrived. Some lasted a week or two, some a day or two — and there was a boy from Dundee who was killed before he could unpack his bag.

Before Dick arrived I was beginning to feel the room had a jinx on it and was about to shift into a small cubicle below the stairs. But there was something about this new arrival that impressed me. He seemed a bit different from the general run of sergeant pilots. He was one of the silent types, although I was soon to learn that this was not a natural

Ready for a shave, Martlesham Heath, spring 1941. Left to right: Bob English, Jack Carmichael, Dick Bruin, Alistair Todd.

characteristic. He had lost his upper front teeth in a training accident and the resultant wide gap made speaking difficult. He would lisp, and when swearing, had trouble pronouncing his f's.

Dick's lanky frame and casual air added a further dimension to the ranks of the squadron sergeant pilots, and although we were soon to share a number of close calls while escorting Blenheims over France, we managed to stay alive and thus widen our flying experience. Most days we would team up as a pair and take turns at leading. Our CO, the bewhiskered Gibb, was a real 'press on' type, and a man of very firm convictions. 'Always stay with your leader Scott. Stick with him no matter what happens. If he flies into a mountain — I expect you to follow suit.' It didn't sound like good arithmetic to me, but with Gibb sergeant pilots were sergeant pilots who, like children, should be seen and not heard.

Dick was always hungry and like most tall boys, never in a hurry. In fact the only time I saw him get a move on was during an air raid. My own bed was set in an alcove or what would be better described as a three-windowed bay, and Dick's was against the wall on the other side of the room. These low-set windows opened out onto a small garden and lawn at the rear of the house. On being requisitioned by the

RAF at the start of the war the house had been stripped of all furnishings including the floor coverings, and a slit trench dug in the centre of the lawn.

To prepare ourselves for any night emergency we would normally leave one of the smaller windows open and during the day practise vaulting off the end of my bed through the opening and onto the grass. Five or six yards on all fours and we were into the slit trench. We soon had it down to a fine art. About four seconds flat. One night we had hardly fallen into our beds after visiting a local pub when the uneven beat of enemy bombers began reverberating overhead. As our ack-ack guns thundered into action so too did the enemy. A stick of bombs exploded some distance away, followed quickly by another that shook the walls of our billet and rattled the roof tiles. I was just about to suggest to Dick it was time we got out when he beat me to it. I could hear his bare feet pounding on the floor boards. There was a bounce on the end of my bed and a crash of breaking glass. Hurriedly pulling on my flying boots, I ran down the passage way and left the house by the side door. Dick had made the trench and seemed oblivious of the fact that he had just sailed through a plate glass window. All he said was 'Jeeze that was a close one'. Once the 'All clear' had been sounded we picked our way back to our room, cold but sober. I thought Dick might have been cut to pieces but the only damage resulting from our forgetfulness was a few superficial scratches and a broken window.

About a week after this incident Dick and I were detailed for a two plane dawn patrol — 10000 feet between Orfordness and Harwich. I had flown it many times before, but in this instance I had an uneasy feeling that something out of the ordinary was about to happen, and was ready and waiting well before take-off time. As I paced the dispersal floor, a mug of tea in one hand and a cigarette in the other, Dick sat on the floor casually pulling on a second pair of grey socks. I asked him sarcastically if we were going to the Pole. He didn't answer immediately. After slowly pulling on his flying boots he stood up, pointed a finger at the ceiling and said 'Scottie, I told my old Mum who knitted these socks if ever I am shot down I will die with my feet warm.' His grin resembled a hangar with both doors fully open. I followed

No. 3 Squadron, Stapleford Tawney, Essex.

him outside towards our Hurricanes, barely discernible in
the pre-dawn light. We were soon off, tucking in our wheels
as we flew over Chesley Petersen's sleeping Eagle Squadron.
To the east the sky was beginning to light the way for a new
day and I could see to starboard the balloon barrage above
Harwich — steel-grey and daunting.

Dick was leading and I positioned myself close in to his
starboard wing to be ready for the unbroken cloud that
covered the sky above. We entered this at 2000 feet and
climbed through into a crisp morning sky at about 6000.
The sun was still under the horizon but as we climbed higher
the cloud below began taking on the appearance of a white
blanket, and the higher we climbed the lighter it became. At
10000 feet the sun burst from below the horizon like a huge
ball of fire. I looked across at Dick. His Hurricane was
illuminated as if by an orange searchlight. It stood out sharp
and clear against the dark blue of the western sky, a picture
of vitality and beauty. I could even see Dick's oxygen mask. It
was hanging free and waggled from side to side as he looked
from left to right. As we dropped our port wings and began
wheeling to the south-west, a sharp staccato voice came
crackling through my earphones. It was the voice of the
Hornchurch controller. 'Hello Spartan leader. Eighty plus

bandits approaching you from zero-nine-zero, Angels 25. Do you read me. Over.' Dick's Midland accent quickly replied 'Roger Clapshaw. Message received. Proceeding Angels 25 on zero-nine-zero.' We opened our throttles to full boost and began climbing hard, the hair on the back of my neck rising to the occasion.

Other friendly aircraft were quickly airborne for I could hear the ground controller vectoring them towards the approaching raiders. We were soon above 20 000 feet and heading for Angels 25. While nearing our target height a squadron of Spitfires appeared. Twelve of them. It was a beautiful sight and I was more than thankful for their climbing superiority as they cruised up ahead of us. Dick began a turn to port and as I followed — my eyes on swivels — I caught sight of a swarm of aircraft directly above us but much higher. The Spitfires must have seen them at the same time for my radio became alive with many voices, some high pitched and anxious, others low and authoritative. I tried unsuccessfully to chip in and warn Dick but he slowly turned on his back and went rocketing downwards. I thought he must have seen some enemy aircraft below us and was racing in to attack. I made sure my gun button was in the 'fire' position and did my best to stay with him. His throttle must have been through the 'gate' for he was going straight down like a bullet. As the cloud raced up towards us my Hurricane began to shudder and I realised we had reached a critical speed and that Dick too must be in trouble. By this time he was well ahead of me and Gibbs' instructions began ringing in my ears. They came through loud and clear like a hammer on an anvil. 'Stick with him.'

My desire to live suddenly took hold of me and in sheer panic I closed the throttle and wrenched back on the control column with both arms, my feet pressed against the rudder pedals. A great weight pressed down on me, forcing my face into my chest and exploding my eyes into what seemed like a million stars. I regained consciousness with my aircraft rolling towards the heavens, the altimeter reading 12 000 feet and climbing rapidly. Although tail-heavy there was no difficulty in bringing her onto an even keel and as soon as I was able to re-set the artificial horizon I asked Debden control for a vector to base. On receiving a course to steer I let down through cloud, breaking out a little to the east of Bawdsey. Martlesham Heath soon came into view and I wasted no time in lowering the undercarriage and dropping onto the grass. While taxying towards our dispersal hut I noticed my aircraft's wings had taken a severe beating. Many rivets had popped and there was a pronounced gap between the wings and the fuselage stub fairings. They had been stretched to their limits. There was no sign of Dick's aircraft and my anxiety was soon confirmed. The observer corps had already reported by phone that an aircraft had crashed at very high speed into the sea off Harwich.

I went back to the bungalow and faced again the agony of losing another room-mate. The broken window had been replaced some days earlier but there were signs of Dick everywhere. His best boots were lying where he had left them in the middle of the floor. There was a half eaten NAAFI bun on a bedside locker and his shaving brush — still white from the morning shave — stood upright in the basin. Apart from a leaking cistern in the bathroom the house was as quiet as a tomb. I sat on my bed as thoughts of the past hour began crowding in on me. The hard climb through the dark cloud into the blazing sunrise. The heavenly arena and its ghostly voices. The screaming power-dive and the rapid return to the

Landing a Hurricane IIc at Hunsdon, summer 1941 (Turbinlight Havocs to right and left in background).

silence of a dull grey room. I began wondering what I was going to say to his mother. She had written to him every day.

At that moment a Rolls Royce Merlin cruised overhead. As it whispered its way into the distance a shaft of sunlight crept through the window. Warm, comforting, like a friendly arm upon my shoulders. It bowed my head and turned my eyes into pools of rain. I had some difficulty finding my forage cap, made my way out the side entrance and quietly closed the door.

On 23 June 1941 No. 3 Squadron moved from Martlesham Heath to Stapleford Tawney, a grass airfield in Essex which came under the control of the North Weald sector. A delightful place, made even more pleasant by the warmth of the summer and the fact that we aircrew were all billeted in neighbouring farmhouses. For two or three weeks we enjoyed the hospitality of our hosts and lived off the fat of the land. But our stay there was all too short. We were suddenly destined to become a night fighter squadron and moved on to Hunsdon, a new airfield in Hertfordshire. Thus began a dark chapter in the history of No. 3 Squadron.

To help combat the German night bombers, a brilliant

No. 3 Squadron at Hunsdon, 1941.

Douglas Havoc II Turbinlite. Note the searchlight in its nose. A barrel-load of batteries that caused more havoc among our own pilots than among the enemy.

part-time inventor by the name of Helmore had come up with the idea of adapting the twin-engined American-built Boston bomber to the role of an airborne searchlight. Aptly named Havoc by the RAF, it was filled with batteries of sufficient strength to operate a high-powered searchlight that was built into its nose. Besides a pilot, it also carried an AI radar operator whose duty it was to direct the aircraft through the night skies onto any blip that was picked up on his screen. Once airborne the Havoc was joined by a Hurricane whose pilot would fall in on either the Havoc's port or starboard wing. This manoeuvre was more simple than it sounds, for the trailing edge of each wing of the Havoc was illuminated by thin strips of concealed lighting. Once the AI operator had homed in on a blip he would order the satellite aircraft by radio to forge ahead and at the same time would switch on the searchlight. In theory the bomber would be illuminated, allowing the Hurricane the simple pleasure of blowing the enemy aircraft out of the sky.

There were two major flaws in Helmore's brainchild. Firstly, with the great weight of batteries, the Havoc was too slow for anything but a sick enemy bomber. The main problem though, was the light. Even on most dark nights there is still an horizon, but once this searchlight was switched on it was so powerful that everything but its target disappeared from sight — the Hurricane pilot's instruments included.

Helmore had sold the Turbinlite idea to Winston

Churchill, who swallowed it hook, line, and sinker. His faith and tenacity outweighed the judgment of those who had to fly the black Havoc or its satellite. Several Turbinlite squadrons were hurriedly formed and much time, life and money were squandered in pursuit of his dream. If I remember correctly, the only aircraft to be shot down by a Turbinlite combination was a four-engined Stirling of Bomber Command!

Twelve months later I was at the mess bar at Bentley Priory, the headquarters of Fighter Command. While

A-Flight, No. 3 Squadron. Hurricane IIc in formation over North Weald.

drinking with some officers of my own rank the question of the Turbinlite was mentioned. I said I thought the nut who had invented it should be locked up in the Tower of London. With that a bald-headed elderly Air Commodore who was standing nearby introduced himself. 'Well Squadron Leader Scott, here I am!' We shook hands to roars of laughter, but I gathered after a lengthy conversation with Air Commodore Helmore that he too had consigned his idea to his office 'OUT' tray. Nonetheless the Turbinlite may well have fed the flame that produced the Leigh Light, Coastal Command's most successful adaptation in its aerial war against the German U-boats.

# Six
# The Hunter and the Hunted

Sleeping by day and chasing Havocs by night was a far cry from the 'circus' operations we had flown above the Pas de Calais or the red-hot shipping strikes along the enemy coast. We felt the war had flown away from us, and I was more than pleased when the great 'Cat's Eyes' Stevens asked for me in person to help him form a night fighter intruder flight at Manston.

Flight Lieutenant Stevens, DSO, DFC of 151 Squadron was already a legend. Much older than most fellow pilots, he had lost his wife and children early in the blitz and his hatred of the Hun was so intense he would fly the night skies from dusk to dawn in search of enemy bombers. He even had long-range tanks fitted beneath each wing of his Hurricane so that he wouldn't have to come down and refuel in the middle of an air raid. He was fearless in attack too, and would often close right in to his target before shooting it down. One enemy bomber literally exploded in his face, spattering its crew's blood onto the wings of his Hurricane.

By this time much of the Luftwaffe bomber force was committed to the Russian front, and raids on England became both scattered and spasmodic. The war became too slow for Stevens. He decided to catch the enemy bombers over their home bases, and so began the partnership of a flight lieutenant and a recently commissioned ex-sergeant-pilot.

Strangely enough our first operation was not carried out by night. An aircraft was known to be down in the sea off Boulogne and Hornchurch operations phoned through to enquire if the experienced Stevens would consider carrying out an air search. An air-sea rescue boat was already in mid-channel and making slow progress towards Boulogne in very inclement weather. Although Manston was almost obscured by fog, his answer was immediate. Yes, we would go and take a look. The 'we' both surprised and frightened me but I was determined to follow him, and hid my anxiety by offering him half a bar of New Zealand chocolate. The way I felt it could well have been part of the Last Supper. We took off in tight formation and lost sight of the ground before our wheels were up. I knew I had to stick with this former airline pilot, for if I lost him my chances of returning safely to base were almost nil. As we turned to port and dropped down over the sea off Ramsgate, the forward visibility began to improve but it was still only marginal.

Within minutes we were off the moles at Boulogne and luckily, after turning onto a reciprocal course, we spotted the dinghy and its crew. Steve gave Hornchurch a fix and we kept it under observation until the rescue craft arrived and scooped it up. I was still hanging onto Steve for grim death and wondering how we were going to make base. Within minutes Steve's wheels were coming down and I quickly followed suit. As the ground came into view I caught a glimpse of a bunker and a putting green and immediately realised we were over the golf course at Sandwich — almost on the south boundary of our airfield. We motored straight in and were soon down safely and taxying towards our

The author and Johnnie Shaw flying Hurricanes above Hunsdon, June 1941.

dispersal area through broken fog. Steve didn't say a word and treated the whole incident as if it was an everyday affair. A few nights later he took off on an intruder patrol to Eindhoven in Holland and never returned. So ended the life of one of the RAF's great pilots. Brave as a lion, and indefatigable. A tremendous example to all who knew him. He was my idol and his loss was a severe and sad blow.

Soon after Steve had disappeared from the scene I was promoted to flight lieutenant — skipping the rank of flying officer — and was given the command of a small band of Hurricane night fighter pilots. Among them were two New Zealanders, Bruce Hay and Peter Gawith.

It was early in 1942 that PO Bruce Hay joined me at Manston. Bruce was five years older than me, powerfully built and with arms like a gorilla. He was also an outstanding rugby player who could pick up a rolling ball at full speed with hardly a stoop. Strong as an ox, he was a good man to have around, whether on the ground or in the air. I once saw him pick an English soldier up by the small of the back and with one arm toss him out the door of a Margate pub. Hardly the correct behaviour for a holder of the King's Commission, but the Englishman had upset Bruce by passing some disparaging remarks about our New Zealand army being pushed out of Greece and Crete.

Not only was he strong but his mind was as sharp as a rapier. One day we borrowed shotguns from the station armoury and were happily hunting hares over a large undulating field to the north of Canterbury. Bruce had just bowled over a hare and was in the act of retrieving it when a middle-aged man riding a heavyweight hunter came belting up towards us. As he reined his steed into a skidding halt alongside, his purple, bewhiskered face began screaming insults at us. What bloody right had we to be shooting on his private property! I tried to pacify the fellow by telling him hares were a major pest in New Zealand and farmers there welcomed their destruction. His answer was that we should take ourselves back to bloody New Zealand — wherever that was — and bloody quickly. Since Bruce and I were wearing battledress, this reply rather annoyed me and I added to my argument by telling him we had both come over 12000 miles to help protect his bloody acres. While I was arguing with the spluttering squire, Bruce had quietly taken the horse by its bridle, undone the chin strap and pulled the bridle off over its head. That done, he swung the dead hare by its back legs in a half circle and gave the horse a mighty clout on the side of its rump. Startled, it exploded off with a fart, a buck and a shower of clods. The rider did well to retain his seat, but lost his hat and riding crop as he hung on grimly to his charger's neck. Just to make doubly sure the horse and rider got his message, Bruce blasted off both his gun barrels into the Kent sky. The horse and its tweedy encumbrance were soon rapidly disappearing down in the direction of a small wood near the far end of the long sloping rectangular field. They vanished into the wood but the horse emerged from the other side, still at full gallop, and minus his rider.

I was never fond of hare and couldn't understand what all the fuss was about. However we took the portly squire's advice, removed ourselves from his broad acres and motored off back to Manston leaving the luckless hare hanging on his roadside fence. This latter gesture of goodwill was wasted, as I noticed when passing by that it was still hanging there — or what was left of it — some three weeks later.

A few nights after our abortive hare-shoot I was nearly knocked out of the saddle myself when flying over Holland. I was taking over an intruder patrol at Gilze Rijen from a Boston aircraft of 418 Squadron, then based at Bradwell Bay, an airfield in Essex. The Boston crew was briefed to leave its patrol area at Gilze sharp on midnight, and I was to take over the patrol at five minutes past, thus giving ourselves a five minute safety-gap over the target area. Soon after I had left the flashing beacon at Willemstad to begin my lonely vigil over Holland, an enemy aircraft switched on its navigation lights and began flying down the airfield's visual Lorenz system which led to a well-lit runway. I dropped into a steep dive but by the time I got myself behind the enemy aircraft I was travelling too fast and had to do a series of S-turns to wipe off some of the speed. By the time I had lined my quarry up he was already on the runway, and as I pressed the firing button and my four cannons thundered into action, both his and the runway lights were extinguished, but the lightning-like effect of a stick of bombs blasted across the airfield to starboard of me. I pulled up sharply to port before shooting past a flak tower that was firing upwards and away from me. I kept fairly low until I was sure I was well clear of the aerodrome defence system, but as soon as I began to climb I was set upon by four very bright searchlights. So bright were these bluish-coloured beams that they completely blinded me, and I had to shut my eyes and bury my head in the cockpit. Fortunately I was too low for them to hold on to me, and was able to make my escape by dropping down still further over the water off the Willemstad beacon. I stayed low while flying between the Islands of Overflakkee and Schouwen, and once past the revolving beacon at Hamstede began to climb again before returning to Gilze Rijen via Bergen-op-Zoom. A large fire was burning on the airfield and I felt sure it was the aircraft I had attacked.

On returning to Manston some two hours later I learnt that the 418 crew had already claimed this German aircraft, but after I put in my own report it was agreed we should share half each — theirs by bombing, my own by cannon fire. A most unusual combination. Some months later we were to learn that neither of our claims was justified. The aircraft that had landed — though damaged — lived to fly another day, but five JU88s were destroyed by fire in a hangar!

It was just as well 418 Squadron had overstayed its patrol, for even if they had scared the living daylights out of me it was undoubtedly their night and not mine. As the great Field Marshal Rommel had said, 'Failure cries out for explanation, but success like charity, covers a multitude of errors.'


I didn't ever bother to find out the name of the pilot who nearly skittled me, and treated it as just another incident in an incident-packed world. Forty years later — and by sheer chance — we were to become great friends.

For many years I had been corresponding with an American friend, Brigadier General Winston Kratz. I had first met Win at Manston just prior to his country's entry into World War II. He had been sent over to England as an observer of our night fighter activities. A quiet, thoughtful man, he mixed freely with all ranks and became a great favourite in all those areas where our night fighter squadrons were based. On America's entry into the war he was promoted to Brigadier General and took command of his country's English-based night fighter force. Win was not only a thorough gentleman, he was also well-heeled, and on retiring from the Air Force at the end of the war, established a very successful thoroughbred stud in Santa Barbara. This industry was also very dear to my own heart, and many letters passed between us over the years. In one I mentioned the incident over Gilze Rijen and he sent a copy of it to one of his ex-pilots, Al Lukas from Charleston, South Carolina. Al, who was — and still is — Editor-in-Chief of their quarterly World War II night fighter journal, turned up his flying log book and proved conclusively that the missing link was none other than himself.

Al Lukas had joined the RAF at the outbreak of war and was flying out of Bradwell Bay as a member of 418 Squadron when he nearly blew me to pieces over Gilze Rijen. Soon after this episode, he had transferred to the United States Air Force and left the United Kingdom for service in the Pacific theatre. I hear from him often, and even after all these years, his letters still remind me of how close I came to death, and how fortunate I am that some hidden force had protected me and saved me from destruction that dark night over wartime Holland.

# Seven
# Manston

To be stationed at Manston was tantamount to camping in sight of Hitler's front fence. Our aerodrome was situated on a small spur of Kent which jutted out into the English Channel near the seaside towns of Margate and Ramsgate, and almost directly opposite the French port of Dunkirk. To the north was the Thames estuary, to the south Pegwell Bay, and that area of the Channel commonly referred to as the Straits of Dover.

Since Manston was so close to enemy territory, it was a natural haven for many a wounded aircraft. Crippled and blood spattered bombers limped in at night, and showers of thirsty Spitfires descended on us by day. After a heavy battering during the Battle of Britain, few buildings were left intact, and consequently most of the station's aircrew were billeted in nearby Westgate. Those of us who lived on the station were catered for in a large old house known as Pouce's Farmhouse. Apparently it had been purchased by the RAF from a Mr Pouce and had served as the Station Commander's residence during World War I. It was old but comfortable, and it also contained the busiest billiard table in the RAF.

In spite of this fragmentation of its aircrew, Manston was a very happy station, and those of us who survived any length of time there became well-versed in every aspect of the air war. All types of aircraft would drop in and add to the congestion of our own Hurricanes, Mosquitos and Swordfish. Great lumbering four-engined bombers — Stirlings, Lancasters and Halifaxes. Twin-engined Blenheims, Wellingtons, Beauforts, Bostons and Beaufighters. These comings and goings put a great strain on our station's services and personnel, yet for all the time I spent at Manston, I never heard one word of complaint. The extra load carried by the engineering and medical sections must have been quite prodigious, but the busiest man in the

Flying a Spitfire, Manston 1942.

whole of the RAF must surely have been Squadron Leader H. J. Smith, our Senior ' Intelligence Officer. Besides recording our own activities which included day and night operations, he had to interview all visiting crews. Whereas we pilots could say our piece and bolt for the mess bar or our beds, Smithy would have to labour on right through the night. The dark shadows under his breakfast eyes were always a grim reflection of the night's activities. A lawyer by profession, he still found time to keep a fatherly eye on us, and his firm but friendly advice saved many of us young pilots from pushing our luck too far. Such men made great stations and Manston was very fortunate to have him as its own.

Although most nights were full of action, one of the worst I can recall was that of 28 August, 1942. Bomber Command aircraft were raiding a number of German cities, including Munich, which was a deep enough penetration at the best of times, but on this night an incorrect wind forecast was given and consequently many of the bombers became short on fuel and thus in deep trouble soon after leaving their targets for the return flight home.

However, Manston's problems began in the early evening when 45 Spitfires of the Northolt Polish Wing descended on us, short of fuel and daylight. One clipped a funnel light and threw the whole Drem lighting system out of commission.

However, once all the Spitfires were settled in for the night, a temporary flare path was set down and the airfield again declared operational.

Our first anxious visitor was a sorely wounded Wellington of 305 (Polish) Squadron. It came in fast with its wheels up and landed on its belly right in the middle of the aerodrome. Several of us pilots jumped into a Hillman van and sped over to the crash, hotly pursued by one of the station's ambulances. The pilot and co-pilot had already left the aircraft by the time we arrived and I gathered from their excited conversation — half in English and half in Polish — that they had been attacked three times by night fighters while on their way to Saarbrucken, and that the rest of the crew baled out east of Dunkirk. This was not quite accurate, for when we shone a torch into the rear gunner's turret its occupant was still strapped into his place of duty. His head was upright, and although his face was ashen, his eyes were wide open and his lips bore a faint smile not unlike the Mona Lisa. The only way to extricate him was by pulling him through the fuselage and out the side hatch. It was as black as ink inside the aircraft as I made my way on all fours towards the tail, still not knowing whether the gunner was alive or dead. A strong smell of perfume permeated the rear turret, a phenomenon not uncommon among Polish aircrew. As our station doctor Squadron Leader Michael Walton directed a torch in from outside, I was able to undo the safety straps and lift the gunner out of his turret and into the body of the aircraft. While doing this my fears were soon confirmed, for although he was still warm, part of his rib cage had been shot away. In my haste to get clear of the aircraft I omitted to uncouple his oxygen supply line and when half way down the fuselage, it snapped and we both finished up in a heap on the floor. I was soon up and hurriedly pulled him out through the side hatch and onto the grass. As Wally ran the torch over him one of his two medical orderlies was sick, and the stretcher which now supported the corpse was lifted into the ambulance by the pilot and co-pilot.

After a shower and change I was back on the airfield in time to witness the arrival of the next visitor. A Stirling came in at right angles to the flare path, narrowly missing the

Wellington and ironing out a Spitfire before crashing into a bay containing an Albercore torpedo bomber, complete with warload. Luckily neither caught fire, the only casualties being the Stirling's rear gunner and the Spitfire. The tail of the huge four-engined bomber finished high in the air, and in his hurry to get clear the rear gunner had baled out of his turret and broken an arm on hitting the ground. The flattened Spitfire had burst into flames on impact, its bright fire illuminating the many Spitfires parked around it. To add to this, several aircraft were circling Manston all calling for emergency landings. Three Stirlings and three Wellingtons made it safely, but another Stirling tried to land too far to the right of the flare path. Several of us were standing by the armoury watching proceedings, when this aircraft made straight for us. We all scattered at high speed and as I became entangled in some loosely coiled barbed wire, I felt its breeze as it ploughed on through the armoury and finished up on its belly near a bellman hangar.

Our own fire-fighting facilities were stretched to the limit and it was found necessary to enlist the services of the Ramsgate brigade. Aircraft still continued to drop in and some crews, running out of fuel, put their bombers down on the sea. By morning 17 badly damaged aircraft had crashed — either on Manston or within sight of it.

Not all night emergency landings at Manston were made by RAF aircraft. From time to time enemy FW-190s and

A captured ME-109.

A captured FW-190.

ME-109s landed in by mistake and their pilots were eagerly pounced on by our own aircrew. There is a bond of fellowship among pilots of all nations and I never saw any animosity towards these unexpected and welcome visitors. In fact our service hierarchy, attending to them as prisoners of war, could never understand why we youngsters enjoyed the company of our captured Luftwaffe opponents. Before they were taken from us they were generally well-stocked with chocolate and cigarettes — luxuries that were not always plentiful in our own squadron dispersals.

An amusing though unusual incident occurred one night when a Mosquito of 23 Squadron was about to become airborne. It collided with a steam roller that had been parked too near the perimeter at the top end of the aerodrome. Although the aircraft was badly damaged the pilot and his navigator were able to leave their cockpit unaided. By the time we reached the crash the navigator was lying face down on the grass and showed no inclination to answer our questions. Squadron Leader Salisbury-Hughes, his thin-faced, bewhiskered flight commander, thinking his subordinate was in deep shock and in need of urgent medical attention, took the morphine injection from his emergency kit and drove the needle into the backside of the prostrate navigator. The reaction was instant. With a loud bellow the patient bounded into the air, almost skittling us in the process. However, it was his flight commander who stopped the flak, for I noticed next morning at breakfast he had quite a lump under his right eye, and his large moustache was a bit sparse on one side.

Such a place was Manston. A front line RAF station which stood without flinching the might of Hitler's wrath. A station which rose from its ashes to become a haven for many a battered and broken soul. Never could my thoughts turn to that small part of Kent without a depth of feeling and a sense of pride, for it was at Manston in the year 1942 that I think I shed my boyhood years and lived to become a man.


My time at Manston ended with the autumn. I was promoted to Squadron Leader and posted to a staff job at the headquarters of Fighter Command. Termed a rest period in aircrew language, it was a time for one's nerves to recuperate from the stresses and strains of an operational tour. I was not overjoyed, yet underneath the uncertainties that my posting notice had brought me, was a feeling that I had had enough. There had been much safer ways of fulfilling an operational tour, but Manston had been so happy and special to us all. On a clear day you could look across the channel and see the enemy coast. The war was on our very doorstep, and the subject of an ever-changing scene.

Stealing alone through the night skies above Hitler's Europe in a single-engined aircraft was an experience that tightened the nerves. My cockpit was an island, a small dot high in the night sky above the edges of the Ruhr. Then there was the battle against the searchlights above the islands of the Scheldt. The heavy flak barrage that seemed to know exactly where you were and which way you were going. The sharp red bursts that sent you racing down to lower levels only to be chased back up again by streams of red-hot tracer. Seeing great cities like Cologne explode, as a thousand RAF bombers emptied their warload from the night sky. The myriads of incendiaries burning like tiny candles way down under. The shattering eruptions of the 4000 pounders. Our own bombers falling in flames or exploding above the target like flashes of orange lightning. The long drag home above a dark and relentless sea. All this was beginning to take its toll.

Peter Gawith, the little New Zealander, and Jerry Shirm from Southport, went missing over Holland on the same night. A few nights earlier Peter had briefly set fire to his own Hurricane while blowing up an enemy aircraft near Eindhoven. He had opened fire at too close a range and when he arrived back at Manston an hour and a half later most of the paint had been scorched off his aircraft. He laughed and cried during his interrogation by Smithy and I sent him on a week's leave in the hope that it would help quieten his nerves.

Mike Marre, who wore the distinctive dark blue uniform of the Royal Australian Air Force, flew into the ground near Ashford on a beautiful moonlit night. Mike with the sandy hair and freckled face. We buried him in the little cemetery at Hawkinge. Bruce Hay, my deputy, was the next to go. Bruce of the long arms and laughing eyes. The brilliant centre three-quarters of the rugby field. He was seen to go

Pilot Officer Bruce Hay's grave, Hawkinge Cemetery, Kent.

down in flames off Dover, at half past one in the morning. I saw it all happen while sleeping on a train which was returning me from Edinburgh to London. I never believed in telepathy, but in this instance it was all so vivid it made me stagger out into the passageway where I was promptly sick.

After arriving back at Manston I searched the sea without success. His aircraft must have taken him to the bottom of the channel for it was not until some days later that his body was recovered by the coastguards from below the cliffs of Dover. He was taken to Hawkinge, an RAF fighter station on the clifftops just behind Folkestone, and I was asked by its adjutant if I would fly over and identify the body. I flew over in my Hurricane and after landing, I let myself down — and Bruce too. I couldn't face the morgue. The adjutant had collected a number of Bruce's little treasures. Under his battledress collar Bruce always wore a rabbit's foot, a miniature silver horseshoe and a small Maori tiki. The adjutant unwrapped a small parcel and there on his desk lay Bruce's three lucky charms. It was a sight that filled my eyes and the best I could do was a silent nod of my head. We buried Bruce alongside Mike Marre. It was a solemn little procession that slowly made its way among the yew trees and the ancient headstones of a nation's past. Nearby were the graves of some of our Luftwaffe opponents — victims of the Battle of Britain. As I saluted my farewell to Bruce, and the bugle's Last Post faded from the scene, I could have been back in the world of Thomas Gray whose *Elegy* had been part of my schoolboy years.

> *The breezy call of incense-breathing Morn,*
> *The swallow twittering from the straw-built shed,*
> *The cock's shrill clarion, or the echoing horn,*
> *No more shall rouse them from their lowly bed.*
>
> ·   ·   ·   ·   ·   ·   ·   ·
>
> *No farther seek his merits to disclose,*
> *Or draw his frailties from their dread abode,*
> *(There they alike in trembling hope repose),*
> *The bosom of his Father and his God.*

Saying goodbye to my Hurricane was like saying farewell to an old and trusted friend. As a young pilot I respected the Hurricane for its quiet manliness. Its ability to absorb punishment, and adapt itself to whatever was asked of it. The sweet purr of its Rolls Royce Merlin engine accepting every challenge without a note of complaint. Its wide, sturdy undercarriage setting you down safely on the roughest of airstrips and on the darkest of nights.

No, there was nothing temperamental about the Hurricane — in fact, I believe there were times when it forgave me my own shortcomings, and while so doing, saved me from an early grave. We had shared the dangerous skies for almost two years. It had flown me safely through flak storms that erupted like multi-coloured volcanoes above our targets in France, Belgium and Holland. The Hurricane may not have had the legs of a Spitfire, nor could it cope so well against the ME-109s in the higher reaches of the fighter pilot's domain. But its versatility more than compensated for its shortcomings. No skittish prima donna, it fulfilled its many roles with a quiet dignity and hard-hitting efficiency.

Operating from French bases, the Hurricane had bravely met the Luftwaffe head on during the battle for France, while a little time later they shot down more enemy aircraft than the Spitfires during the Battle of Britain. But that was not all. After the Battle of Britain the Hurricane had become a valuable jack of all trades, readily adapting itself to the dictates of a well-meaning, but often misguided RAF hierarchy. 'Put bombs on it' was the order from Air Ministry, and it became a 'Hurribomber', carrying a similar load to a twin-engined Blenheim bomber and with much greater accuracy and efficiency. Mounted on cargo ships it became known as a 'Hurricat', and was catapulted off short rusty decks to do battle against the German four-engined Condors that often shadowed our Atlantic convoys and the sea lanes that led to Murmansk. A brief moment of glory before parting with its pilot as they both headed down towards a deep and cruel sea.

In the Western Desert campaign, some Hurricanes acted as airborne artillery, mounting two anti-tank guns — one under each wing. And while the Spitfires slept on their native heath, the Hurricanes kept a night vigil above a bruised and battered Britain. But it was the arrival of the airborne rocket that gave the Hurricane its greatest punch. With its four 20 mm cannons and eight 60 pound rocket projectiles, it was to become the scourge of enemy shipping — particularly those vessels that tried to run the gauntlet of the English Channel or among the islands of the Scheldt.

The Hurricane's versatility therefore knew no bounds, yet as it became the recognised low-attack work horse of the RAF, its glamour as a fighter aircraft sadly diminished. The Spitfire on the other hand climbed higher and higher into the comparatively safe and less productive arena above Hitler's Europe.

I lowered myself into the cockpit of my Hurricane for the last time on the evening of 9 August 1942. Not to fly. Just to say a quiet thank you and goodbye. The north star was already shining as if lighting the way to the heavens where we had spent so much of our time. It was strangely quiet too, as I thanked God for delivering us both from the perils of the past. It was a difficult parting and I felt saddened as I let myself down to the ground and slowly made my way through the deepening twilight towards the noisy comfort of Manston's officers' mess.

# Eight
# Staff Officer

Saying goodbye to Manston was also like saying farewell to an old friend. More so perhaps, since I was a little apprehensive of my new appointment. I'd had no experience of staff work, nor had I been among the brighter pupils at my Grammar School. To be posted to the headquarters of Fighter Command at Stanmore was sending me far beyond the boundaries of my youth. My few brief brushes with the staff at 11 Group HQ at Uxbridge had already put me on the defensive. The non-flying-types in their various little empires had led me to believe that higher education and flying were worlds apart. They treated us pilots with an air of superior indifference, and we didn't have to be told that in their view it was only birds and fools who took to the air — and most birds had the good sense not to fly at night. They spoke well and had a repertoire all their own. You could hear them in the bar, at the dining table, and in the stand-up part of the loos:

'I couldn't agree with you more old boy. You sound so like Freddie!'

'Dear old Freddie. The last time I saw him was in the Sudan. Mounting a camel if you please.'

'Good heavens! No!'

It was not my scene, and I could only surmise that the staff at Bentley Priory would be much the same only on a much grander scale.

On arriving at the Priory I was soon to discover that my fears were largely groundless. On entering the mess bar I was greeted by Laddie Lucas, Barrie Heath, Johnnie Kent and Duncan Smith — all wing commanders of great distinction. All pilots with the one burning ambition — to get to hell out of the place and back on operations. We formed ourselves into a tight circle, drank too much and made ourselves scarce at every opportunity. Not only did we find some of the regular staff hard to understand, we also had to contend with the antics of a number of elderly army and naval officers who had been recalled from retirement to serve as liaison officers for their respective services. I soon ran foul of two old naval captains who would persist in fighting the 26-year-old Battle of Jutland on the mess bar. They would set up their line of battle, corks and bottle tops for the lesser craft and jugs and ashtrays for the capital ships. These battles always got off to a calm beginning but usually finished with one or the other wiping the two fleets into the scuppers. I briefly became a naval hero in the eyes of the bar stewards when I arrived in the middle of one such engagement. A little the worse for wear after visiting Shepherds pub in the Haymarket with Don Parker, I picked up a soda syphon and let fly at the neatly arrayed fleets, skittling three destroyers and a flagship in two short squirts. Even the barman who caught the wash forgot his place and roared with laughter. Not so the navy. The two old captains appeared to have been struck by lightning.

'I say Scott old man. You can't do that. That's the Rodney!'

Our Commander-in-Chief was Air Marshal Sir Sholto Douglas. He had succeeded Sir Hugh Dowding when the latter had been relieved of his command after the Battle of Britain. In appearance Sholto Douglas was not unlike Göring,

Bentley Priory, headquarters of Fighter Command, situated in the London suburb of Stanmore.

his opposite number in the Luftwaffe. I didn't see a lot of him, but what I did see left a lasting impression. He was a strong supporter of all his pilots and had a great memory for faces and places. He was also a keen follower of the game of rugby and even surprised me by phoning my office and asking if I would like to accompany him to Twickenham to see the annual match between the Navy and the RAF. We pilots on the staff at Bentley Priory felt we had a strong ally in Sholto Douglas, but it was not to last. After I had completed two months of my rest period, he was posted out to the Middle East and replaced by our old chief of 11 Group days, the controversial Air Marshal Sir Trafford Leigh-Mallory.

I could never understand why certain senior members of the RAF spoke so vehemently against Sir Trafford. Pompous he may have been, but I think this was due to a certain measure of inner shyness. Like all successful commanders, including Sir Keith Park, Leigh-Mallory had his service adversaries, but he also had his admirers. He was very supportive of all who flew and was held in high regard, particularly by all squadron and wing leaders. As illustrated in my book *Typhoon Pilot,* there were times when I too experienced the sharpness of his tongue, but unlike Sir Keith Park he never held any resentment towards his subordinates or those with whom he disagreed. In fact the opposite was the case, as the following extract from a letter I recently received from American General Matthew Ridgway confirms.

While not a pilot, I took every opportunity to fly in just about every type of fixed aircraft (and helicopters too) in the U.S. inventory, starting with a Navy seaplane in 1915. Then my WWII service was capped as Commanding General U.S. 82nd Airborne Division through Sicily, Italy, and Normandy, and then of the U.S. XVIII Airborne Corps on to the Baltic.

Through all those years up to 1955 when I retired, I thought you might be interested in a brief of my association with the flying fraternity, and specifically with that gallant and talented airman and charming gentleman, Air Marshal Sir Trafford Leigh-Mallory. I came to admire him greatly during the numerous pre-Normandy planning conferences concerning my Division.

The mark of his character for me was his manliness in one incident, and his thoughtfulness of a subordinate in another.

Up to the last he had strongly urged Eisenhower to cancel the proposed drop of the two U.S. A/B Divisions because of his belief that it would result in the 'futile slaughter' of these two great fighting units.

Eisenhower, Bradley and the two Division Commanders all strongly urged the drop, as worth the risks involved.

Afterwards, when it became clear that both Divisions had landed without too heavy losses and had contributed markedly to gaining lodgement as planned, Leigh-Mallory went at once to Eisenhower, stating that no one could have been more distressed than he at the time, to have added to the burdens of the Supreme Commander nor happier now that Eisenhower was right and he, Leigh-Mallory, was wrong.

On D-1 Day I received a hand-written note from the Air Marshal sending his best wishes for our success and expressing his admiration for our gallantry. It struck a warm note to which I replied hours before take-off.

In post-war writings, much weight has been placed on Sir Trafford's invitation of Squadron Leader Douglas Bader to a meeting of the Air Council. Few writers seem to understand that we in the RAF were still learning at that time, the members of the Air Council included. Who better to voice his opinions than Douglas Bader — a pilot with up-to-the-minute experience? Leigh-Mallory was big enough to acknowledge this, which is more than I can say about some members of the RAF's hierarchy at that time. If Sir Trafford offended the Air Council by the 'Bader incident', so too must the wily Churchill have done. Only 16 days after he was made Prime Minister, he asked to see a lowly flight lieutenant — Max Aitken (Lord Beaverbrook's son), so that he too could become familiar with the conduct of the air war. As Max has said in the *Aitken Papers*:

Naturally I knew that I had not been ordered to London in the middle of a battle simply in order to be given a good meal. Before I knew where I was, I was being subjected to a severe cross examination. The Prime Minister wanted to know how things were going with fighter squadrons. He was not a man to be satisfied with official stories filtered through the various levels of Air Ministry.

The only fault I could find in Sir Trafford Leigh-Mallory — if it was a fault — was his insistence that all pilots posted to his HQ Staff on rest must serve there for the full six months.

Life behind a desk was like being back at school, and there was no escape. On each desk were three wire trays, each with its own *In, Pending,* and *Out.* In theory, the *In* tray would be full of files in the morning, dealt with during the day and consigned to the *Out* tray by late afternoon. Any files containing subjects that took some time to answer were consigned to the *Pending* tray and dealt with at my leisure — generally after the evening meal and often well into the night. It was a problem that always worried me, for it was not uncommon to see a stack of files a foot high in my *Pending* tray while the other two were empty.

My immediate boss was Air Commodore Basil Embry whose office was just across the passage way. Basil was already a legend and one of the few officers of Air Rank who actually flew operationally. Shot down over France, he had made his way back to England, and without the help of the Underground. He hated staff work as much as we did and he would often poke his head into my office and say in his clipped English, 'What are you up to Scottie?' I would resignedly point to the load of bumph in the *Pending* tray. 'Stick it in the wastepaper basket, we're off to Shepherds.' Since an order was an order I gladly obeyed and crammed myself into Basil's Humber staff car alongside five or six other officers. It broke the monotony and did much towards helping us to prepare ourselves for another operational tour.

We were also encouraged by Leigh-Mallory to visit as many stations of his command as possible. Since this included the whole of England, Scotland and Wales, including the Shetland and Orkney Islands, there were many stations to cover. Unless instructed to visit a particular station I generally confined these activities to those stations more familiar to me, which mainly lay along the south coast. Quite often, visits to familiar squadrons had their rewards. One

Chalky White.

evening I dropped into Westhampnett — an airfield near
Chichester — to see 485 New Zealand Spitfire Squadron,
and was invited to stay and attend a party in the sergeants'
mess. I had hardly entered the building when Dumbo Grant,
the Squadron CO, introduced me to a powerfully built
sergeant pilot whose shoulders were so wide they appeared
to be bursting out of his battledress. Sergeant Leslie
McQueen White — or Chalky as he was better known — put
out a hand that resembled a smoked ham and felt like the
blunt end of a stable broom. Clutching my own hand in a
vice-like grip he treated my arm as if it were the village
pump. While my fingers screamed out for mercy, a broad
smile crossed his face, pushing his eyes into two slits and
reminding me of a picture I had once seen of an Eskimo
chieftain. I was thankful when he released his grip and
reached out across a well-stocked table for a bottle of beer.
No fancy tools were necessary. He casually pulled the cap off
the bottle with his teeth, took a long swig and after a hearty
belch handed me what was left of its contents. 'Cheers,' he
said in a gravelly voice. He didn't wait for my thanks, as two
sergeant pilots began a heated argument on the other side
of the table, and Chalky without further ado detached
himself from Dumbo and me and moved off in their
direction. I couldn't hear what was said above the noise of

the party, but the two misfits, on being spoken to by Chalky quickly disappeared — and in different directions. With my hand still smarting I had good reason to feel impressed, nor was there any need for Dumbo to remind me who the boss was in the sergeants' mess at Westhampnett.

Chalky looked more like a lumberjack than a Spitfire pilot, although I was not surprised when Dumbo said he came from a sheep farm in the Waikaka Valley in Southland. I could immediately picture his tousled head and long arms in the shearing shed, and the sweat, pain and blasphemy of the high country muster. He would have left school about the same time as I had — in the mid-thirties, that hungry period in our New Zealand history often referred to as the Depression, or the Sugar Bag Years.

Some weeks later I met Chalky again. It was in Kings Lynn, a town in Norfolk, where I had been attending an afternoon cinema show. I was without my car and joined a long queue which was attached to the last bus of the day that could take me to the RAF station at Sutton Bridge where I was to stay the night. One glance told me that even with a bit of luck, my chances of a bus ride were slim. The queue, made up of civilians and service personnel, was three or four persons wide and about 30 yards long. Chalky and another sergeant pilot were several places ahead of me, and further ahead still was a tall, thin middle-aged woman who kept complaining about the pressure being put on her from behind. This appeared to be generated by a handful of army types who had obviously been celebrating in a local pub. The complainant, on having her hat knocked askew, threatened the British Army with a furled umbrella and attempted to elbow her way forward a place or two. This was not a popular move on her part, and caused some dissension among her fellow queue members. Chalky, full of initiative, reached forward with a long arm through a forest of legs and pinched the woman in the rear. She let out a scream, leapt in the air, and swung her umbrella smack across the ear of a nearby soldier. The innocent recipient and his mates had good reason to feel offended. One grabbed the umbrella and broke it across his knee, and before you could say 'Home James' the queue had forgotten the bus and had transformed itself into a round riot. Soldiers and civilians set to in noisy haste. Not Chalky — nor his mate — nor me either. Feeling like a long-tailed cat in a roomful of rocking chairs I quickly followed my fellow New Zealanders onto the bus and sprinted upstairs to the top deck where I was able to command a bird's-eye view of the frenzied scene below. Those who were wise enough to untangle themselves followed us onto the bus and the driver, sensing a load of trouble, quickly put his vehicle into gear. As we drew away from the kerb, quite a sizeable land battle was taking shape. Some of the combatants were on the footpath, some on the roadway, while two were wrestling in the gutter alongside a telephone booth.

The cause of all this was still in the centre of the argument but by this time she had lost her hat and glasses, and her hair, previously in a bun, had come adrift and was behaving like a grass skirt in an Hawaiian hula. Chalky, comfortably seated up front, didn't even look behind. He sat talking to his fellow sergeant as if the situation he had left behind was none of his business. He saved me a long walk, and as the bus bounced along the road to Sutton Bridge, I couldn't help thinking what a fine type Chalky was to have around in times of need.

If we missed the squadron spirit at Bentley Priory, we made up for much of our loss by frequent excursions into the West End. Whether in pubs, clubs or backstage in many of the London theatres, we were spoilt to such an extent that we often found it difficult to make our way home.

Barrie Heath, Johnny Kent and Duncan Smith were posted out to the Middle East, presumably at the request of Sholto Douglas, who was already established in his Cairo office. I was sorry to see them go, for each in his own inimitable way helped to make life a good deal happier than it might have been. I was particularly sorry to see Johnny go. A friendly and forthright character, he had put up a tremendous performance while leading the Northolt Polish Wing in the Battle of Britain. Johnny had been awarded a DFC and Bar and the Polish Virtuti Militari, their highest decoration, but if any man deserved a DSO from a grateful British nation it was this man from Canada. Somewhere along the way his forthrightness had got the better of him and he had crossed swords with a senior officer, and unhappily paid the price. This was no isolated incident. Similar treatment was meted out to another outstanding pilot — Squadron Leader David Douglas-Hamilton who served under Sir Keith Park in Malta. David had completed over thirty deep PRU (photographic reconnaissance unit) penetrations into enemy territory, all unarmed and unescorted, at a time when the loss rate on such missions was horrific. He had a brush with Sir Keith, and finished his tour and returned to England without so much as a mention in dispatches. He was killed two years later after bringing a crippled Mosquito back from Germany. His aircraft had been hit by flak which knocked out one motor and critically wounded his navigator. He almost made it but not quite. He crashed and was killed while approaching Benson, the PRU base in Oxfordshire. After a long period of operational flying he passed from this world undecorated.

Air Vice Marshal Arthur Gould Lee summed up his feelings when he wrote after the war:

I have never been able to fathom why the VC was not more often awarded, not for one act of desperate courage but for scores of cold-blooded courage, such as, for example, those performed by determined Bomber Command crews in their hazardous tours of duty, and in Fighter Groups by intruder crews doing comparable work but singly by both night and, especially when we had long range fighters such as the Mustang, by day.

Canadian Wing Commander Bob Braham was a typical example. By the end of the war he had received three DSOs and three DFCs and in my view, anyone who can sustain this level of valiant achievement over many months, is worthy of the VC. Nearly all his victories were gained at night, and over enemy territory.

He could have added to this such names as Wing Commander Johnnie Johnson, an outstanding pilot and wing leader who had shot down 38 enemy aircraft — all fighters! Johnnie's performance was not the result of a brief skirmish. Each victory was gained after a period of hair-raising combat similar to the hand-to-hand fighting of the First World War, with each pilot's life very much at stake. Add to the list such a man as Douglas Bader. Flat feet didn't stop him from serving in the armed forces.

The RAF was very much the junior service in such matters. That status was even more pronounced among members of the Dominion aircrew. Once seconded to the RAF they came under the jurisdiction of its Air Ministry and took their place on equal terms with their English crew-mates. Our British Chief of Staff was not under the dictates of New Zealand's Prime Minister Fraser as was General Freyberg and his New Zealand Division. Nor were we subjected to any inner circle, nor sheltered by a watchful and benevolent Brigadier Kippenberger. Nearly 11 000 New Zealanders were scattered among squadrons of the RAF. Four thousand failed to return. Had such figures prevailed in the New Zealand Division during its Middle East campaign it would have created a political storm. Many questions would have been asked in high places, yet of all those New Zealanders who served in the RAF, none would have had it any different. The great comradeship that grew under the stresses of the air war created a human amalgam which has stood supreme in the hearts of all who served in the flak-torn skies above Europe.

# Nine
# Return to Operations

My term as a temporary staff officer came to an end on a rather auspicious date 1 April 1943. Sir Trafford Leigh-Mallory had kept his word and I was posted to Tangmere to take command of 486 (NZ) Squadron. A comparatively new squadron, it had been formed 12 months earlier at Kirton-in-Lindsey as a Hurricane night fighter squadron before re-equipping with Typhoons.

In spite of its late entry, it was to finish the war as New Zealand's top-scoring squadron. Outstanding in its versatility and in particular, in its role as a fighter bomber squadron. However, all this was yet to develop, whereupon it cast its dark shadow upon all areas of the Luftwaffe's domain.

The Typhoon was a recent addition to the RAF's armoury. Like all new aircraft it had its teething troubles. So many in fact, that had Göring not set his fighter bombers against the coastal towns of southern England it may well have been thrown out of production. When its 24-cylinder, 2500 horsepower Napier Sabre motor behaved itself it could move the Typhoon along faster than any aircraft at that time — the ME-109 and FW-190 included. If its motor was temperamental, its tail section was even more so. It was not uncommon for them to snap off.

In my book *Typhoon Pilot* I refer at some length to my first meeting with a Typhoon:

> Whereas the Spitfire always behaved like a well-mannered thoroughbred, on first acquaintance the Typhoon reminded me of a half-draught; a low-bred cart horse, whose pedigree had received a sharp infusion of hot-headed sprinter's blood. . . .Mastering it was akin to subduing the bully in a bar-room brawl.

I was pleased to read Richard Hough's similar description in his splendid book *One Boy's War.*

S.A.K. Typhoon 1B of 486 Squadron flown by 'Spud' Murphy above Tangmere. Note the old type cockpit canopy compared to the bubble hood fitted to D.J.S. (see page 83).

To take off a Typhoon was to grapple with a low-bred all-in wrestler, and the thud of the wheels tucking into the belly after take-off was like the sound of the bell at the end of the round. At first, every take-off, however, strenuous, was also a victory; every landing a world war triumph.

For all its faults the Typhoon, once it had settled down, was to become the greatest low attack aircraft of the Second World War. Tough, pugnacious, uncompromising it might have been, but loaded with bombs or rockets it became the nightmare of the Wehrmacht's skies.

Tangmere, situated near Chichester on the south coast, was much like Manston in its performance. It was the equivalent of a jack-of-all-trades. Not only did it cater for its two resident wings — one of Spitfires and the other of Typhoons — it also acted as host every moon period to the special service aircraft. These were a mixture of Lysanders and Hudsons employed on cloak-and-dagger-operations. They would land in France and conduct a two-way exchange of secret agents. Tangmere also provided a haven for many a crippled bomber. Lancasters, Halifaxes and Stirlings were frequent visitors.

Outside B-Flight 486 Squadron, Tangmere, summer 1943. This garden and lawn were set out in one night, 'borrowed' from a local farmer. Nearest the camera are (left to right) Allan Smith, Frank Murphy, Ian Waddy and the author.

Much is made of Biggin Hill, due I think to the fact that it was a straight-out fighter station, very close to London and the eager attention of the press, but it could never be compared with such stations as Manston or Tangmere and their round-the-clock performance.

I was no stranger to Tangmere. I had landed there often when shut out by the weather from Manston or on staff visits to its squadrons. A pre-war station, its living accommodation was like that of a first-class hotel. Unfortunately this was in direct contrast to the squadron dispersal areas. Whereas the officers' mess and the ground staff accommodation were built in good solid English brick, the squadron dispersal huts appeared to be very much an afterthought — and a hurried one at that. Flimsy wooden buildings, each heated by a pot-bellied stove and furnished with a table and a few old tattered armchairs. If this wasn't primitive enough, behind each hut stood a single lavatory, a tall thin contraption that had obviously borne the weight of many a squadron briefing. Painted on a door, which was swaying on one rusty hinge, was a notice for all prospective patrons. 'Peasants keep out. This is where the nobs hang out.' As Arthur Umbers showed me over the rest of his B-Flight complex I made a mental

486 Squadron, Tangmere 1943, grouped on and around a Typhoon S.A.F.
On prop: Jimmy Cullen, Frank ('Spud') Murphy, Rangi Swinton.
Sitting on wing: J.R. ('Sandy') Powell, N.W. 'Fairy' Fairclough, R.H.
('Fitz') Fitzgibbon, R.J. ('Bluey') Dall, J.A. ('Froggie') Frogatt, D.G. Fail,
K. McCarthy, A.E. ('Doc') Jones, Norm Preston, L.J. ('Happy') Appleton,
R.J. Dansey, Norm Gall, N.S. Parkes.
Standing: A. ('Arty') Sames, M.O. Jorgensen, H.N. Thomas, W.B.
Tyeman, Group Captain Crisham (Station Commander), the author, Ian
Waddy, Allan Smith, J.G. ('Woe') Wilson, H.C. Seward, G. Thompson.

note to have the lavatory door repaired, and a shorter and
more appropriate notice affixed.

Flight Lieutenant Harvey Sweetman commanded A-Flight.
He had flown Spitfires with 485 Squadron and was the most
experienced member of my new command. 486 Squadron
had remained on the defensive since its formation but I was
soon given permission to take it onto the offensive. We had
bomb racks fitted to all our aircraft and were soon winging our
way over to France, each carrying 1000 pounds of bombs.
These alongside our four 20 mm Hispano cannons made
quite a formidable armoury and we wasted little time in
returning to our opponents some of the treatment they had
been dishing out to the towns along the south coast. In fact, in
bombing their airfields we took from the Luftwaffe more than
our pound of flesh. St Omer, Poix, Tricqueville,
Beaumont-le-Roger, Bernay and Caen Carpiquet were all on
our visiting list and we showed them no mercy. Nor did we

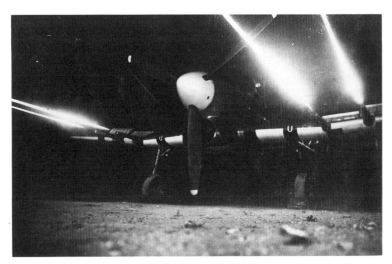

The four 20 mm cannons of Typhoon D.J.S. being tested on the butts at night, Tangmere, 1943.

allow their ports to go unmolested. Le Havre, Cherbourg, Boulogne and Dunkirk received their fair share of attention, particularly in our war against the E-boat flotillas of the Bay de La Seine. To add to all this we still managed to knock down our share of hit-and-run raiders and act as close escort to the medium day bombers of 2 Group. It was to be a busy and dangerous summer but 486 Squadron lived up to its Maori motto, 'Hiwa Hau Maka' — 'Beware The Wild Winds,' and became one of the most respected squadrons of the RAF.

By this time too the Typhoon had mended its ways, and although we lost many pilots when pressing home attacks through the flak storms surrounding their targets, only one was lost through a fault in his aircraft. Since most of these operations were at low level we were unconsciously setting a pattern that was later to be adopted by all Typhoons of the 2nd Tactical Air Force. In attacking ground targets with cannon fire, rockets and bombs the Typhoon reigned supreme. No longer were our armies at the mercy of the lumbering metal giants of Hitler's Panzer Divisions.

Soon after my arrival at Tangmere, Group Captain Paddy Crisham took over as Station Commander. In the service you met many fine characters. Paddy is one who stands out in my memory and the following words always remind me of him.

I pass through this world but once. If therefore there be any kindness I can show or any good thing I can do, let me do it now. Let me not defer it or neglect it for I shall not pass this way again.

Once I had the squadron into full stride, and attacking a wide variety of targets in France, I was asked by 11 Group HQ if I could take under my wing a flight of American Thunderbolts — the idea being to teach their pilots some of our methods of low attack operations.

The pot-bellied Thunderbolt was not unlike the Typhoon in some respects. Powerful, large and heavy, it would have made a suitable American wife for its British counterpart. The Typhoon had the edge over it low down, but the Thunderbolt excelled in the higher altitudes. The pilots' attitude was a refreshing change from the stiff upper lip normally displayed by the British, and they mixed in well with my New Zealanders — so much so that they could have been one of us. Their lack of experience and naivety about Service etiquette caused us many a chuckle, but they were as keen as the proverbial mustard and made up for these deficiencies in many different ways. They were also great tellers of stories. I shall never forget a leather-faced lieutenant from Texas who came up with the following — and without so much as a smile.

'An elderly couple were driving on a main highway in Florida when an elderly State patrolman stopped them for speeding. The woman was hard of hearing and when the patrolman began talking to her husband, she kept asking "What did he say? What did he say?" The patrolman's first remark was "Did you know you were doing over 65 miles an hour?" The wife tugged at her husband's sleeve and asked "What did he say?" Patiently her husband repeated the patrolman's remarks. Then the patrolman asked to see his driving licence. The wife asked "What did he say?" Again the husband repeated what had been said. After looking at the driver's licence the patrolman said "I see you are from Charleston South Carolina. I've been there. In fact the ugliest woman I ever dated in my life came from Charleston." The wife asked "What did he say?" "He said he thinks he knows you dear."

485 and 486 Squadron crests.

Hank Meyer was à great character and I was sorry to hear he was killed in his Thunderbolt a few days after leaving Tangmere for his home base in Norfolk. How his fellow pilots fared is something I never knew. They were a cheerful bunch and brought many a ray of sunshine into some of our darker hours.

It may sound strange to the reader, but seldom did we give much thought to the human element when fighting our adversaries. Our thoughts were certainly centred on the enemy aircraft, but the pilot's cockpit was only a small part of it and our success or failure rested on the death of the aircraft itself. If the pilot was lucky enough to bale out, only then did we give him a thought. One of the few times I came face to face with my opponent was on the morning of 14 April 1943 near Cap d'Antifer in the Bay de La Seine. He was flying a ME-109 and I was fortunate enough to creep up on him from below and behind without being seen. One short burst from my cannons at close quarters blew his canopy off and stopped his motor. I could see he was in deep trouble and decided to formate with him as he made a shallow dive

The author leading his Typhoons off on a dive bombing mission from Tangmere, summer 1943.

towards the sea. I could clearly see the horrified look on his face, for he had shed his helmet as he tried to lift himself out of his cockpit. To add to his difficulties I slid in behind and gave his aircraft another burst of cannon fire. Both he and his aircraft hit the sea at the same moment and quickly disappeared under a huge fountain of spray. That second burst of my cannons was neither wise nor necessary. A spur of the moment action that even to this day still troubles me deeply. Detlef Walter was born in Kreuzburg/Oppeln on 17 March 1921. A German pilot whose terrified young face will haunt me for the rest of my days.

Attacking enemy E-boats in the Bay de La Seine was among our primary objectives. Thin skinned they might have been, but they made up for this deficiency by carrying a large number of 20 mm and 37 mm guns. As with our attacks on German airfields, it was like flying into a hornets' nest. Their most dangerous weapon was the quadruple 20 mm cannon which for some reason or other we called a 'Chicago piano'. The volume of coloured tracer sent up by the E-boat flotillas was a frightening spectacle and our chances of collecting a packet were very much in the enemy's favour. One such attack was carried out on the evening of 14 September. We ran into them as they were leaving the Seine

Shrapnel through the port wing of a Typhoon.

estuary. It was the largest flotilla we had yet encountered and I was quite surprised to see a fleet of some 15 E-boats taking to the open sea without any sign of air cover.

I led the squadron in a wide sweep to seaward, well clear of their flak and the heavier shore-based guns, and at the same time kept my eye open for enemy fighters. Most 20 mm and 37 mm guns were fed by belts or magazines and since they all opened fire simultaneously they also required re-charging at approximately the same time. It was during this comparative lull that I ordered the squadron to attack. We swept in low in a full-blooded cannon onslaught, each sorting out his own target. I went in low on one of the flotilla leaders and as my cannon fire ripped into it there was quite a large explosion amidships and the E-Boat spun around in a tight circle and stopped. Another boat to starboard of it was being strafed by my number two, PO Fitzgibbon. As I swung around, hotly pursued by a large volume of tracer, I could see the crew of another boat taking to the water. They dived into the sea in all directions and were quickly swallowed up in a heavy concentration of cannon fire which whipped the sea into a white frenzy. Frank Murphy set his sights on a flak ship that was accompanying the flotilla and must have scored a hit in its magazine, for there was a terrific explosion which left it listing to port and on fire. By the time we had completed two

A-Flight pilots outside dispersal hut, Tangmere 1943.
Back row: D.G. Fail, W.J. Swinton, G. Thompson, J.R. Cullen, H.N.
Thomas, H.C. Seward, M.O. Jorgensen, R.J. Dall.
Front row: A.W. Sames, W.B. Tyeman, C.N. Gall, I.D. Waddy.

attacks, many of the boats were stationary and smoking, while others scattered at high speed towards the protection of their shore-based guns.

I was relieved when calling the squadron together to find none were missing, although on landing back at Tangmere we discovered that several aircraft bore severe wounds and one ground-looped because of a punctured tyre. Three days prior to this engagement we had caught a single E-boat as it was about to enter the moles at Le Havre. It must have been transporting a party of German soldiers from either Ouistreham or Trouville to Le Havre. I stopped it dead in its wake with my first burst and was surprised to see it was loaded with troops who took to the sea in haste. The E-boat was a sorry sight by the time my eight Typhoons had finished with it, and the sea surrounding it had been churned into a white lather which didn't show much promise for those German soldiers who had sought the protection of its waters.

Although discouraged by most station commanders, nearly every operational squadron had its dog or dogs. My own dog was a wire-haired terrier by the name of Kim. Some were

In the cockpit of D.J.S., the first Typhoon to be fitted with a bubble canopy. The author's dog Kim thinks it a good idea.

owned by individual pilots, others had been adopted by the squadron — legacies from the death of their owners. Fred was already in residence when I took command of 486. A small, chocolate and white, short-haired, long-tailed mongrel who treated our squadron dispersal as if he were its landlord. After falling over him a couple of times I had to remind his owner, Arthur 'Spike' Umbers, who was in charge of B-Flight, that although I was very fond of dogs, I preferred to risk my neck against the enemy, and his dog should be made aware of this.

After my sharp reprimand, Fred must have got the message, for thereafter he kept well clear of me and always seemed to look on me with a marked degree of suspicion. One morning after returning from a red-hot shipping attack near Le Havre, I was sitting in my office trying to enjoy a few shaky puffs from a cigarette. On looking out the window I noticed Fred had set himself up on the edge of the tarmac taxi-way and was busy at his morning toilet, head down and one hind leg at twelve o'clock high. He was happily engrossed when there was a loud report from behind the dispersal hut. He gave a high-pitched howl and shot into the air as if struck by lightning. After flicking around in a few tight circles he made off, weaving rapidly and without a backward glance, in the direction of the officers' mess. I leaned out the window to follow his noisy progress and saw at once he was heading fast for further trouble. A hundred yards towards A-Flight dispersal a Typhoon at right angles to the taxi-way was straining at its chocks while being run up in a full blast engine test. Well over 2000 horses from its 24-cylinder Napier Sabre engine were driving the huge three-bladed propeller at maximum revolutions, creating a slipstream fierce enough to topple an elephant. When Fred was hit by this wall of compressed air, it looked as if he had been side-swiped by an express train. He disappeared like a chocolate-and-white catherine wheel in the direction of the station's barbed wire boundary fence.

I didn't see him for some days after this incident but he finally turned up at our Squadron's dispersal hut bearing a pronounced limp and still very much the worse for wear. I asked Umbers what had caused his dog to join the jet set but he preferred not to comment. He did however, pass some caustic remarks about our sheep farmers, of whom there were several in the squadron, but other than that, I had to leave things to my own imagination. I noticed however, that as soon as the shotguns appeared for practice clay bird

A pranged Spitfire at Gilze Rijen. A ground staff member illustrates how the pilot finished up — bruised, a few cuts, but fit enough to fly the next day.

shooting, Fred would take off in noisy haste, and in whatever direction his nose was pointing.

He was to share the joys and sorrows of our Tangmere summer and although he continued to treat me with distant respect, he became so much part of squadron life that I was pleased to accept him as a member. If our tails were up, so was his, and in our sorrows he was always among the mourners.

I posted Umbers off operations in the autumn and didn't see him or his dog again until some twelve months later. By this time I was commanding 123 Wing — four squadrons of rocket-firing Typhoons then based at Gilze Rijen in Holland. While leading a low attack mission on the German border town of Wesel I was hit by flak and force-landed on Vokel airfield. The first person to meet me was Umbers. He had finished his rest period and was now back on operations commanding 486 Squadron, which was part of 2nd TAF's 122 Wing. As he drove me from my aircraft towards the squadron dispersal hut I saw Fred standing in the snow near the doorway, his eyes focused on our arrival. He showed no sign of affection — or indeed recognition — on our approach, and quickly disappeared into the warmth of the hut.

Umbers offered to drive me back to Gilze Rijen and I gladly accepted, for that morning I had received the startling news that the Germans were gathering their forces in preparation for an assault across the Maas. This breakthrough was aimed at Antwerp and I preferred to be back in command of my own wing as soon as possible since Gilze Rijen was in a direct line between the Maas and Antwerp.

We had much to talk about during our drive. Most of the boys who had flown Typhoons with us at Tangmere had been killed or were prisoners of war. As the jeep hummed along the Dutch highway and the dark trees of evening melted into night, our conversation became interspersed with long periods of silence. I was quietly contemplating what might have been my own fate a few hours earlier over Wesel when I felt a cold muzzle at the back of my neck, and a warm tongue briefly licked my ear. A moment of canine affection that may well have been a message of farewell. I begged Umbers to stay the night but he had an early morning show to lead and was taking off next afternoon for England to visit his wife and new born baby. After dropping me off at Gilze Rijen, Spike and his dog set off on their return to Vokel. I never saw either again.

Umbers was killed next morning. Shot down by flak while attacking barges on the Dortmund-Ems Canal. I mourned his loss. We had shared many a tight spot when flying out of Tangmere in the long summer of 1943. I shed a tear for his little dog too. A faithful camp follower who had given his squadron everything he had. A mongrel dog who played his own important part during a crucial stage in the history of a war-torn world.

# Ten
# A New Weapon
# Appears

As the summer advanced and the momentum of our
operations grew to a crescendo we suddenly found ourselves
confronted with two strange new targets. One was a
self-launching flying bomb which Hitler named the V1. The
second weapon, known as the V3, was more like an orthodox
cannon, only its shell-like projectile was fired from a 400 foot
barrel by a system of separate charges piped into the barrel
at frequent intervals. This gave the warload a tremendous
velocity, and with 50 barrels mounted in a huge concrete
dome-like structure near Mimeyecques, all pointing at
London, one could visualise the tragedy this new weapon
could bring upon the capital.

Hitler was well aware of their potential and the heavy flak
barrage surrounding them bore out his wicked testimony. All
Typhoon squadrons were converted to 'Bombphoons' and
we threw ourselves at these strange sites in what could well
be described as the second battle for Britain. Sixty-nine V1
sites had been photographed from the air in the Pas de
Calais, and two V3 sites — one in the Pas de Calais and the
other at Martinvast on the Cherbourg Peninsula. The V1
sites were not easy to find, in direct contrast to the V3 sites,
which gave themselves away. We learnt through our secret
agents that the V3 site at Mimeyecques was surrounded by 56
heavy, and 76 light anti-aircraft guns. They were without
doubt the most formidable targets we had ever had to face.
By this time I had been promoted to Wing Leader of the
Tangmere Typhoons and on the first occasion, while leading
486 and 197 Squadrons against the V3 site at Mimeyecques, I
could see in my dive that our attack with 500 pound bombs
was a dangerous waste of effort. Bomber Command was later
called in and the whole site plastered with their heaviest
bombs. Thanks to them, the V3 never got off the ground and

thus London was saved the torture of round-the-clock bombardment.

The V1 sites were less easy to eradicate and tied up a large part of Bomber Command, the 8th Air Force and the 2nd Tactical Air Force before they were overrun by the Allied Armies in September 1944 — three months after D-Day. It had been a costly departure from the orthodox method of air warfare from both the German and Allied points of view. More so the Allies perhaps, for it diverted their heavy bombers away from the strategic bombing of Germany — a change in plans that may have prevented a much earlier end to the war in Europe. This diversion also cost the RAF well over 2000 aircrew, more than four times the number that had been lost in the entire Battle of Britain.

Although we continued to hammer hard at flying bomb sites for the rest of the summer, we also managed to pay plenty of attention to enemy shipping and the airfields of our Luftwaffe opponents. As the year drew towards its end, so too did my operational tour. I was posted to command Hawkinge. I would be temporarily out of the battle but certainly not out of the firing line. Hawkinge was the closest station to France and had been subjected at times to heavy shelling from across the Straits of Dover. Unlike my posting to Bentley Priory I didn't feel entirely out of my depth, for just prior to my posting to Hawkinge I had commanded Tangmere for two weeks while Paddy Crisham was away on leave.

One afternoon during this period I had a phone call from Flight Lieutenant Griffiths asking me if I would be interested in an evening pheasant shoot. Lyndon P. Griffiths was one of the great characters of the New Zealand Air Force. We had joined the Air Force at Levin on the same day. He had left his school desk to walk straight into a very dangerous future. Griff belonged to one of the Spitfire Squadrons on the other side of the airfield from 486. He was a big boy with a permanent smile and an uncommonly high-pitched voice. In earlier days while flying on the same sweeps over France I would often hear his voice over the radio. Sometimes it was accompanied by wolf whistles from pilots of other squadrons. One afternoon he was shot down over the Channel and before leaving his aircraft gave a high-pitched and anxious commentary on his predicament, his Wing Leader repeatedly chipping in and ordering him to bail out. Someone else suggested he loosen his braces. It was not until his Spitfire was dangerously near the sea that he climbed out and used his parachute. His last message before he hit the silk was a high-pitched 'Jeez. It's going to be cold.' The crew of the naval launch which picked him up was too liberal with the rum and when Griff was delivered to Manston after coming ashore at Ramsgate he was highly intoxicated, dressed as a sailor and telling us all to go and get ourselves shot down.

When he phoned me about the pheasant shoot I was occupied with a visitor from 11 Group HQ and accepted his invitation without question. He picked me up at my office at the appointed time and we set off in the direction of Sir William Bird's estate. The Sussex countryside was well stocked with pheasants, and some senior officers were often invited to shoot over neighbouring properties.

Griff's idea of pheasant shooting was quite new to me but not wishing to spoil his fun I threw myself into the spirit of the chase. His old car had a sliding hood and while Griff drove, his two passengers stood up — torsos through the hatch — each armed with a double-barrelled shotgun. On sighting a bird over the roadside hedges we would take aim. If successful, Griff would leap out of the car, retrieve the bird and throw it in the boot. After he had picked up about a dozen, a one-armed man stepped out from a hazel hedge, stopped our car and asked Griff if we had been shooting pheasants. Griff, with an air of injured innocence replied that nothing had been further from his thoughts. Not convinced, the man went around to the back of the car and flung open the boot. A squawking cock pheasant, which must have only been winded, flew out in his face and nearly knocked him over. Griff didn't wait for an explanation and set off at high speed in the direction of Chichester.

Next morning there was a message waiting for me in my office: would I please phone Sir William Bird. Bearing in mind that attack was the best means of defence, I contacted him immediately and greet him head on. 'Yes Sir William. To what do I owe this pleasure?' After beating about the bush for some time he eventually came to the point. He didn't mind inviting colonials to his country estate for organised shoots but he strongly objected to New Zealanders waging a mechanised all-out war against his private property. Three Air Force officers wearing New Zealand shoulder-flashes had been apprehended by one of his gamekeepers. Would I please carpet them and take the necessary action to see that it didn't happen again. Only recently one of his gamekeepers had lost an arm when a passing Canadian Bren-gun carrier had taken a pot shot at one of his pheasants. A bullet had ricocheted off a post and shattered his left arm above the elbow.

I apologised to him on behalf of the three New Zealanders and said I would take appropriate action. We finished up on good terms and he even invited me to an organised shoot on the following Sunday, but I thought it wiser to advise him that I had a prior engagement.

I was sorry to leave Tangmere. 486 and 197 Squadrons had grown into a tightly knit Wing. Their versatility, whether on the field of play or in our missions across the Channel, left little time for contemplative leisure and their high morale and popularity did much towards keeping Tangmere among the greatest stations of the RAF. Nonetheless, it is just as well that youth is resilient and can recover quickly from the hair-raising experiences associated with an operational tour. Often we could be surrounded by laughter while having our after-lunch coffee and within little more than half an hour be hammering into an E-boat flotilla in the mouth of the Seine or weaving through the murderous flak barrage of an enemy airfield. It was shattering to see our Typhoons crashing into the sea or exploding over the target. Yet for all my time as Squadron and Wing Leader at Tangmere, not one of my pilots buckled under the strain. In 1982 at a post-war reunion of 26 486 Squadron pilots who had flown from Tangmere, 16 had been shot down — and two of them twice — all by flak.

My last trip as Wing Leader almost ended in disaster. I was ordered to take the two squadrons on a dive-bombing mission to the V3 site on the Cherbourg Peninsula. Just as I was about to roll over and head down to the target a burst of heavy flak exploded under my port wing almost knocking my Typhoon onto its back. As I continued on down through a wall of flak my heart began thumping like a steam hammer and I was more than thankful when I completed my dive and was able to head out to sea above the quiet waters of the Bay de La Seine.

As Tangmere Wing Leader I had been fortunate to have under my command 197 and 486 Squadrons. Any formation is generally only as good as its commanding officer. If the CO sets a bad example in the air or on the ground, you can bet your last shilling his squadron pilots will follow suit. If, for instance, a Squadron Commander struts around the officers' mess wearing a scarf instead of a tie, or with maps hanging out of the tops of his flying boots, his subordinates are sure to behave likewise. If a squadron is untidy on the ground, this is generally reflected in its performance in the air. I was lucky with 197 and 486. Both squadrons maintained a very high standard. Although a jovial man, Jacko Holmes who commanded 197 was a stern taskmaster, and his squadron personnel simply worshipped him.

To have command of a RAF squadron was undoubtedly the apex of one's service career. Like a headmaster you were in direct command of your pupils and staff — your pupils

The author's Typhoon being refuelled at Tangmere, 1943.

being the pilots, the staff, the squadron's ground personnel, that happy band of assorted tradesmen affectionately known in the service as Erks.

In my own case I was in an even happier position, for all 486 Squadron's pilots were fellow New Zealanders. Our ground staff were predominantly British, but we did have a small spattering of New Zealanders among the squadron's wireless mechanics and armourers.

A Squadron Commander could make it his duty to know every member of the squadron by name, and as I have said, its performance in the air and on the ground was a reflection of his own example. A good squadron was always a happy one, and the cooperation and depth of friendship that developed between the pilots and those who served on the ground was also a true reflection of the state of the squadron's administration.

When promoted to Wing Commander Flying, much of this camaraderie was lost, for I was then very much on my own, my duties more or less being confined to leading the squadrons and working in close harmony with the Squadron and Flight Commanders of those squadrons that made up my Wing.

A Group Captain's life was even more detached, for the weight of the station's administration allowed little time for operational flying, and visits to squadron personnel were normally confined to those aircrew briefings that were held before and after the Wing's operations.

I posted several 486 Squadron pilots on rest before my departure from Tangmere. Two, 'Woe' Wilson and 'Bluey' Dall, wished to be repatriated to New Zealand. This I arranged, but no sooner had they returned to their native shores when letters began to arrive in quick succession. Would I please pull every string within my reach to have them posted back to the United Kingdom! According to their plaintive pleas, New Zealand was no place for aircrew who had flown in Europe, as square-bashing and other forms of elementary drill were apparently more important than flying. These requests put me in a quandary. Both pilots had acquitted themselves well in their tour with 486 and I felt it my duty to give them both my support and the assistance they so richly deserved. On the other hand, I could not guarantee their survival if they returned to the United Kingdom for another operational tour. I replied to this effect but they would consider no alternative and after more pressing letters I had them flown back to England in a Liberator of Transport Command, much to the surprise and chagrin of those New Zealanders who had treated them like wayward children.

On their return to England Woe was posted onto Typhoons and was shot down by flak a few days later. He survived, but received no less than 65 pieces of shrapnel in his body. Bluey was less fortunate. I had him lined up for a job ferrying Mustangs out to Shaibah in the Persian Gulf. Unfortunately he borrowed a Typhoon, flew over to the Continent and killed himself while performing a series of aerobatics in front of some of his friends, his aircraft crashing and bursting into flames. I had been speaking to Bluey only a day or two before his death. He was so full of life and profoundly grateful for my having rescued him from what he termed 'the New Zealand Home Guard'.

Bluey was actually an Australian, having joined the RNZAF while on a working holiday in New Zealand. A typical Australian, he would bet on two flies crawling up the window. His leisure hours in 486 at Tangmere were spent either at the races with Paddy Crisham, or scanning the racing pages of our daily papers. While at Tangmere, Bluey had become friendly with the Duke of Norfolk who had news of a very promising colt entered in the Derby of 1943. Bluey couldn't see Booby Trap being beaten so we packed him off to Newmarket in the station's Tiger Moth, loaded down with our bets. In racing terms there is an old saying, 'On the turf and under it, all men are equal.' With this, Bluey could never agree, and being a born optimist, he was invariably broke. However, his faith in Booby Trap was as firm as the Rock of Gibraltar and he flew off to the Derby leaving us all certain that we were onto a good thing.

Booby Trap must have blown his fuse well before the half-way mark for he finished his race stone motherless last. On hearing the result I thought Bluey might delay his return to Tangmere because of engine trouble, but not so. He returned next day full of smiles and bonhomie. So full, in fact, that I quickly gained the impression that he had hedged our bets and had done very well for himself by backing the winner — Miss Dorothy Paget's bay colt Straight Deal. I still remember this colt well. By Solario out of a mare named Good Deal. Booby Trap, who was owned by Lord Derby, was later shipped out to New Zealand to stand as a sire, but his performance in this field was no better than his efforts in the English Derby. Whenever I saw any of his progeny running in the post-war years, I immediately thought of Bluey — but I made sure none of his runners carried my money.

One could never leave an operational command without a feeling of deep emotion. In sharing the perilous skies we had depended so much on one another that we became closer than brothers. Our lifestyle had re-shaped our thoughts and destinies as nothing else ever could. We had in some ways outlived our youth and become hardened professionals. The loss of a squadron mate was still hard to bear but we accepted it as a matter of course and simply drew closer within ourselves.

# Eleven
# Hawkinge

Hawkinge could have been a smaller edition of Manston. It took care of two resident Spitfire squadrons (501 and 322), but I still wasn't entirely finished with Typhoons. Lympne, ten miles to the south-west, also came under my command, and stationed there were many of my former friends who were serving in Nos. 1 and 609 Typhoon squadrons. Both were top squadrons and already well versed in the art of low attack.

501 Squadron flew Spitfire Vs and its pilots were employed almost solely on reconnaissance along the French and Belgian coasts. Commonly referred to as 'Jim Crow' patrols, they would seek out targets for our fighter and torpedo bombers.

501 was commanded by a young Wellington accountant named Garry Barnett who, looking for something more exciting than an office desk, had joined the RAF in 1939. A pleasant, smiling chap, he had previously served in 485 Squadron, when he was shot down over France while on a fighter sweep. After bailing out safely near Amiens, he made a very determined bid to reach Gibraltar. Caught and imprisoned near Nice, but still undaunted, he made a dramatic escape and reached Marseilles under his own steam. From there he was able to make contact with the Underground movement whose members helped him over the Pyrenees, through Spain and on to Gibraltar. Garry Barnett was made of stout stuff, for after being flown back to England he immediately re-joined his squadron. I was pleased to have him as CO of 501.

322 wasn't formed until June of 1943. Unfortunately their inexperience outweighed their enthusiasm and consequently their brief time with me at Hawkinge was mainly restricted to training sessions. Major K. C. Kuhlmann, DFC — a South African — was an excellent CO, and once his squadron was re-equipped with the Griffon-engined Spitfire Mark XVIs, it

acquitted itself well enough against Hitler's secret weapon the V1, shooting down $108\frac{1}{2}$ (their best effort by FO Brugwal, who destroyed five in one day).

Once the Allied Armies had overrun the V1 launching sites along the French coast, 322 Squadron was again re-equipped, this time with Spitfire XIs.

It was a painful transition from shooting down 'doodle bugs' (flying bombs) to operating as fighter bombers. On the first day of September, and on the one operation, they lost their CO and both Flight Commanders — all by flak.

I had been in command of Hawkinge for only a few days when it was time for the monthly mess party. These parties took the form of a dance and buffet supper and were held on the evening of the first Sunday in each month. It wasn't the happiest of times for a commanding officer as one had to spend most of the evening entertaining local dignitaries, many of whom were old enough to be my parents. Some of the male guests had served in the Royal Flying Corps in the 1914-18 war and it was polite for me to be interested in many a long-winded combat that had taken place over France in those far off string and canvas days. Supper time was a welcome relief, as most guests were soon busy in reply to the padre's Grace. The cooks and mess staff excelled themselves at these parties, as did the aircrew. The tables were laden with pheasant and partridge supplied by the pilots who spent their spare time shooting the countryside for anything that wore fur or feathers.

After picking my way through a small portion of partridge and potato salad, I moved into the dance hall for a much-needed cigarette. The floor was deserted save for a cluster of appreciative young women who were being entertained by a junior officer at the far end of the floor. Contrary to regulations he had shed his tunic, rolled up one trouser leg and was doing the Highland Fling in time to the mess orchestra. At some stage his shirt tail had come adrift and much to the amusement of his female admirers, it was flapping at the back of his trousers.

Presently I was joined by the performer's Flight Commander who, sensing at a glance that I was not amused, hurried over to his subordinate and in no uncertain terms ordered the young offender to remove himself from the dance floor. This advice seemed to take some time to sink in, but when the Flight Commander pointed to the young blade's shirt tail the reaction was immediate. He quickly tucked the offending garment in, took a horrified look in my direction, leapt onto the stage and disappeared behind the orchestra. Some of his fellow officers were beside themselves with laughter. I was about to say something to steady them up when I became stuck for words. After looking hard at my shoes for a moment or two I made my way outside and had a good laugh under the moon.

A few nights later it was my turn to make a fool of myself. The officers' mess at Hawkinge had suffered severely in the Battle of Britain and what was left of it was not quite large enough to accommodate both squadrons. 322 was a Dutch squadron and its officers were quartered in a fine old manor house some miles from the Hawkinge airfield. Lympne had already put on a welcoming party and the Dutch, anxious to please, had organised one of their own. I was a little late, and the party was in full swing by the time I arrived. As soon as I stepped in the front door I had a glass of Bols thrust into one hand and a plate with a raw herring on it into the other. The herrings were a gift from Queen Wilhelmina and from the way her subjects were diving into the barrel, it was quite obvious they were a rare and much sought after delicacy. However, this delicacy was new to me and according to the proverb 'When in Rome do as the Romans do' I took a sip or two of Bols, raised my chin and lowered the silvery fish by the tail and began to chew. It could well have been a dish cloth soaked in fish oil and my first reaction was to get rid of it and quickly — but by this time I had an interested audience. I was surrounded by a circle of Dutch pilots munching herrings.

Without insulting my host there appeared no avenue of escape and I simply had to keep chewing. After quite a struggle I managed to down it with the help of my gin, but no sooner was it tucked away than it began to behave like a yo-yo. Not knowing where the lavatory was, I excused myself on the pretext of wanting to collect some cigarettes from my car which was parked at the front door. Once outside I dived for the shrubbery where I spent a miserable half hour getting rid of the Dutch Royal Treat.

Shivering and exhausted, and attempting to remain as inconspicuous as possible I quietly let myself back into the party by way of the rear entrance. In the corner of the room I had so hurriedly vacated, and where most of the revelry was taking place, sat a large parrot or cockatoo in a plain wire cage. I couldn't let myself immediately back into the spirit of the party for I was no longer in the mood — nor could I face the sight of another raw herring. The bird was a welcome diversion and I began my re-entry by trying to make friends with this unhappy-looking, narrow-faced squadron mascot. He remained half asleep and I put my right index finger through the wire cage while trying to attract his attention. I was preoccupied with this when someone tapped me on the left shoulder, and I half turned towards a Dutch officer who was offering me another glass of gin. As I went to take it in my left hand there was a loud squawk, and I felt as if an express train had run over my right index finger. I tried to pull it clear but the parrot's sharp hooked beak was snapped into it like a red-hot vice. Blood started to squirt in all directions and I couldn't get free until a quick-thinking

No. 322 (Dutch) squadron crest.

Dutch officer picked up a soda syphon and gave the parrot a short sharp burst in its face.

It was a most unhappy party from my point of view, for the finger wouldn't stop bleeding and I finally had to excuse myself and return to Hawkinge where the station doctor repaired the damage, which left a scar I carry to this day. Had I been wise enough to study the Dutch squadron's official crest I would have saved myself this bloody embarrassment. In its centre was a parrot, and under it the motto, 'Niet praten maar doen' — 'Don't prattle, act'!

Hawkinge was a busy station and I enjoyed being its commanding officer, but the mounting activity in all areas of the south coast made me realise if I stayed too long in my job I would be missing out in the struggle for Europe. Even in midwinter the whole of the south coast was springing to life. Many new airfields, set out and grassed in the previous summer, were now being occupied by skeleton staffs, all working like beavers preparing to receive the squadrons of Coningham's 2nd TAF.

Each airfield was designed to accommodate a Wing and each Wing comprised from three to four squadrons — plus all the ground components and paraphernalia necessary to support them. Like the Desert Air Force our Wings had to have wheels — hence the title Mobile Wing. A Wing was in fact a mobile station and contained all the elements of its static counterpart. Moving, of course, was much easier. All the personnel and servicing echelons of a Mobile Wing were accommodated under canvas and shifting from one part of England to another, although quite a mammoth task, was relatively simple in its execution. When a move was on, the ground staff were split into two groups with both halves being quite capable of servicing the squadrons. The 'A', or forward party, would move to the new base and quickly set up shop to cater for the arrival of the aircraft. Once these had flown in, the rear or 'B' party would pack up and move forward to rejoin the 'A' party. It was as simple as that but required approximately 300 assorted vehicles, mainly three-ton Bedford trucks, to carry it out.

My two Typhoon Squadrons were withdrawn from Lympne. No. 1 Squadron went to Martlesham and 609 joined 198 Squadron at nearby Manston. I felt as if I had

99

Commanding Officer of 123 Wing in July 1944, aged 25.

been robbed and didn't like to see them go, but I knew that 2nd TAF would be extracting more than two teeth from the vast armoury of Fighter Command. It came as a surprise — though not an unpleasant one — when I received notice to relinquish my command of Hawkinge and proceed to Manston to take command of 123 Wing. At the age of 25, to command four squadrons and a Mobile Wing seemed a little beyond my reach. Not only was 609 Squadron to be back under my command, I also had 198, 164 and 183 Squadrons — all rocket-firing Typhoons of great renown.

609 and 198 Squadrons were already well known to me, mainly through my earlier association with Manston where both squadrons had spent most of their operational time. 164 and 183 were comparatively new squadrons. 164 being formed on 6 April 1943 at Peterhead, and 183 on 1 November 1943 at Church Fenton. However, both squadrons had made up for their late arrival and were already well versed in their work as low attack rocket-firing Typhoons.

609 was an auxiliary squadron that had been formed in 1936. Known as the North Riding Squadron of Yorkshire, its versatility was much like 486's. But unlike 486 Squadron whose pilots were all New Zealanders, not one pilot in 609 was a Yorkshireman. Most were Belgians. Good keen experienced pilots who were a joy to have under one's command.

Regrettably, over the following 12 months when 609 remained under my command in 123 Wing, five of their commanding officers were shot down by flak. Five experienced young leaders the Wing could ill afford to lose.

I wasted little time in handing over Hawkinge to my successor and made my way to Manston by road. Long before arriving at the main gates I could hear the deep growl of many Typhoons as they were being warmed up ready for another foray across the Channel. Rough, tough and uncompromising they may have been, but it was a sound that set my blood alight. A sound which became so deeply etched in my memory that it is as audible to me now as it was in those far-off days of my youth.

123 Wing's crest.

# Twelve
# Wings On Wheels

Returning to Manston was like going back to my old school, although I was sorry to learn that two of my favourite station officers had left on promotion to other commands.

Without Smithy and Wally, Manston could never be quite the same. However, as a Group Captain I had been promoted above the rank of its station commander and became so involved in the business of 123 Wing I found little time to become interested in Manston's own domestic affairs.

I suffered a sad blow soon after my return to Manston. While visiting nearby Margate, my little dog Kim was stolen from my station wagon. It was like losing a child. He had been such a bright spark in my life and he in turn had depended so much on me. To make matters worse, he went missing on his first birthday. I spent many a sleepless night wondering as to his whereabouts — whether he was chained to a cold kennel, or kept warm and well-fed in the way to which he was accustomed. I prayed for his return, but I was never to see Kim again.

Five days after taking over my new appointment I was ordered by 84 Group HQ to move the squadrons down to Thorney Island, a large airfield near Portsmouth. The whole move went like clockwork and the four squadrons never missed a beat. They were operating against V1 sites in the Pas de Calais from Manston in the morning, and flying on the offensive from Thorney Island in the afternoon. In moving the equivalent of a small town I thought there would be a number of problems but there were none. Every department of the Wing conducted its transfer in true professional manner. It was the first of many moves but I was already convinced I would have no fears about our mobility or in facing up to the demands of Operation Overlord and its commitments to our crusade through Europe.

Thorney Island was the ideal place to knit the Wing into one big happy hard-working family. For the first few weeks the squadrons were kept busy attacking V1 sites, targets that went under the code name 'Noballs'. Whoever invented such a name for these targets deserves some credit, for it never ceased to create a certain amount of ribald humour among the pilots whenever the name was mentioned during their briefing sessions.

2nd TAF provided me with a large semi-collapsible three-roomed caravan, mounted on a six-wheel Austin chassis. It was austere but comfortable and its driver, who was also my batman, could have it ready for occupation within a few minutes of its arrival. Not only did it provide my sleeping quarters, it also served as my office, and the extra room I used for accommodating visiting friends. I also insisted that it be parked near the briefing complex which comprised two similar caravans separated by a large marquee. It was a highly mobile set-up, for I also kept my Typhoon near my caravan plus the two Austers of our communications flight. Added to this was my own personal staff car — a large V8 stationwagon.

RAF Station Thorney Island was separated from the mainland by a narrow waterway and small wooden bridge. Prior to the war it had been a general reconnaissance aerodrome and although our Typhoons were to appreciate the long concrete runways, all members of 123 Wing were now under canvas. So its many permanent brick buildings were generally occupied by the station's permanent staff on a more or less care and maintenance basis.

Hampshire was one of my favourite parts of England, and often, to rid myself of some of the pre-invasion tension, I would take to the skies after breakfast in one of our little Austers and do an aerial cruise around the county. I enjoyed these early-morning excursions and found it much easier to settle into the day's office routine after hedgehopping around for half an hour or so.

Some mornings I would invite one of my administrative officers to accompany me. We sat side by side, and their reactions to low-level flying varied considerably. Most took it in their stride, but some of the older men would be quite satisfied with the one trip and always found some lame excuse if they were invited a second time. Wing Commander Munson was one such officer. 'Mun', a most delightful man, had retired from the regular Army some years prior to the war and had re-enlisted in the RAF for airfield defence duties. During his Army career he had been a champion pistol shot and taught me all there was to know about handling a long-barrelled Smith and Wesson. So well in fact, that I was soon to head him off at target shooting — a victory which he confided to me gave him the greatest pleasure, but which I knew caused him much embarrassment, particularly when he was constantly reminded of it by other officers of my Wing.

One morning I asked him to fly with me on a low-level tour around the Sussex countryside. Since he was always telling me of the dangers of life on the Somme during the First World War I purposely kept very low to see what effect those far-off days might have had on his nerves. We skimmed over hedges and slipped between tall trees. I saw him shut his eyes as we flew straight for a big red barn, and his legs and body stiffened as we flew under some power cables. The Auster I was flying had recently had an engine overhaul and although the oil pressure gauge was registering the required pressure there was a strong unpleasant smell of hot oil and I thought it wiser to cut our trip short and return to base. As I switched off the engine after arriving outside my caravan I apologised to Munson for the brevity of the trip and added that I didn't like the smell of the motor and asked him if he could smell it too. 'Smell it? Cripes, I think I'm sitting in it.' He never flew with me again.

Another morning I landed an Auster in a field behind our motor transport section and climbed through a hawthorn hedge to say good morning to Flight Lieutenant Short, our Cockney transport officer. His tent was situated midway along two lines of three ton Bedford trucks and as I walked towards it I could see his batman was on guard but facing away from me, his eyes glued to the main entrance. He was a tall thin boy, and when I suddenly surprised him from behind with a loud 'Good morning Buick' he spun round awkwardly and became very agitated. 'Where's Short?' I asked. Buick pointed towards the tent entrance but was so embarrassed by my unexpected presence he was unable to give a coherent reply. I peered into the tent which smelt of stale beer and found Short still in bed. He looked up at me through bleary bloodshot eyes and began putting on a death scene that would have done justice to a Shakespearean actor. There was a field telephone alongside his bed and I reached down and phoned through to my Wing sick-quarters, advising the duty doctor that we had a very sick transport officer on our hands and would he come quickly. Within a few minutes Flight Lieutenant Bell arrived. I intercepted the doctor before he had time to dismount from his jeep and quietly asked him to give Short the usual checkover and if all was well, to give him two or three 'number nines'. Since even one of these laxatives was strong enough to move a reluctant concrete mixer, I had a feeling Short would soon be up and about and well occupied for the rest of the day. After Bell had administered the medicine I put my hand on Short's brow and informed him that it might be in his best interests if he remained in bed for the day and also added that I would be back later to see how his recovery was progressing.

I returned in the late afternoon. Buick was still on guard at the tent's entrance, but Short's bed was empty.

'Where's Short?' I asked

'He's not 'ere Sir'

'Well where the hell is he Buick?'

'He's on the loo Sir. Been there most of the day Sir. Real crook 'e is Sir.'

Some days later after finishing an inspection of Short's transport empire I found reason to compliment him on the general tidiness of his vehicle dispersal. A true Cockney, he was fully recovered and very much his pint-sized, irrepressible self.

'Thank you Sir. Kind of you to mention it Sir.'

With that he saluted me and added a rider.

'Cor blimey Sir, that young Dr. Bell didn't 'arf set me alight. Didn't really need to go near the loo. Could 'ave hit it from 'ere Sir.'

With that he pointed to a scrim-covered object set in the hedge some thirty yards beyond his tent site. I must have appeared puzzled for he became quite agitated, saluted me twice, and hurriedly opened the door of my stationwagon.

As I drove away I noticed the faithful Buick was still staring fixedly in the direction of my dust, while Short was heading fast for the little house in the hedge.

# Thirteen
# The Politics Of War

Prior to leaving Tangmere for Hawkinge, I had become friendly with Britain's Foreign Secretary Mr Anthony Eden. His country retreat, Binderton, was not far from nearby Chichester and we would often gather there for a game of tennis. Mr Eden took great interest in my New Zealand squadron and I thought it would be a nice gesture if he were offered the Honorary Air Commodoreship of 486. Winston Churchill was serving a similar position in 615 County of Surrey Squadron. Mr Eden was delighted to accept, but unfortunately my proposition didn't receive the same enthusiastic response from New Zealand's Prime Minister Mr Peter Fraser. He apparently didn't think it appropriate for a New Zealand squadron to have a Tory Air Commodore while he was the country's Labour Prime Minister. Hence our meeting at Thorney Island shortly before the Wing's departure for Normandy was far from amiable. It was the first time I had met our Prime Minister. It was also my first taste of politics, and although disappointed, I had to forget the incident which soon became lost in my workload.

I came to know Mr Fraser much better when he visited the United Kingdom at a later date. He invited me to dine with him at the Savoy. I don't know what prompted him to issue this invitation, for most of his guests were members of England's new post-war Labour Government. The only exceptions were Mr and Mrs Bill Jordan, our High Commissioner who I guess had every right to be there, and myself — a young group captain who could speak of nothing but the war.

This dinner was held in the Prime Minister's private suite. Mr A.V. Alexander, the First Lord of the Admiralty, was seated on my left at the head of the table, and opposite me were Mr Fraser and Ellen Wilkinson, who I believe was Minister of Housing in Attlee's Government.

I took an instant dislike to the First Sea Lord, for when he

A group of 485 Squadron pilots standing by a Spitfire MK9B with Sir William Jordan, New Zealand's popular London High Commissioner.
Left to right: J. Ainge, L.S.M. (Chalky) White, L.P. Griffiths, M.R.D. Hume, N.E. Frehner, Bill Jordan, M.G. Sutherland, B.E. Gibbs, H.S. Tucker.

referred to the British Navy he would say 'his Navy' this and 'his Navy' that. As far as I was aware, this gnome of a man had never been to sea in his life, having been elevated to his civilian honorary title through the rough and tumble waters of party politics. In his younger days he had served briefly as a private in the army and also as a Baptist lay preacher!

During the meal he asked me what I thought of his Navy — and in particular its support of Overlord. Since quite a number of RAF aircraft had been shot down by the Senior Service I was pleased to be able to oblige and give him my honest appraisal. He glared at me, stopped eating, stood up and thumped the table.

'I won't have you criticising my Navy like that Scott!'

I looked across at Mr Fraser. He was regarding me over the tops of his spectacles and shaking his head. I felt an angry flush come to my face, but let the matter drop and turned my attention to the roast beef.

Mr Alexander sat down, but didn't speak to me again and it was only after I received a sly wink from Mr Jordan some minutes later that my composure was partly restored.

After Mr Fraser's parliamentary guests had departed I had

485 (NZ) Squadron, Selsey, May 1944. In black and Homburg hat is Mr Peter Fraser, Prime Minister of New Zealand. The author was about to fly him to Thorney Island. Bill Jordan, our High Commissioner, is in the middle of the front row.

a lengthy discussion with him on the future role of the RNZAF. With the end of the Pacific war in sight I could see little future for Dominion air forces if they were allowed to revert to their pre-war composition. Keeping abreast of the scientists would be a very expensive commitment and the only solution as far as I could see was to retain a Commonwealth Air Striking Force such as the RAF was at that time. Each member of the Commonwealth would contribute financially on a pro rata basis and modern squadrons would be based in rotation in every Commonwealth country. Thus we would achieve that degree of mobility and flexibility so necessary in modern warfare. Under this scheme the RNZAF could still retain its static elements which would assist the mobile servicing echelons belonging to the visiting squadrons. Aircrew would become familiar with the earth's geography and ground crews with the maintenance of modern jet aircraft.

The wartime RAF was in fact a Commonwealth Air Force. Eleven thousand New Zealanders served in its formations alongside Australians, South Africans, Canadians, etc. Mr Fraser deflated my enthusiasm when he said such a programme would be impossible due to the ever changing political differences within the Commonwealth. Throughout the war years they must have held a truce, for at no time did I ever hear politics discussed. We were like one large family, all pulling our weight and operating like a well oiled machine.

I could see there was no point in pursuing the matter with the Prime Minister. He did, however, restore some of my dignity by saying he very much regretted the difference I'd had with the First Lord of the Admiralty, and added that I was not to feel discouraged as there would be ample room in the post-war world for men who were prepared to stand by their convictions. Since he was prepared to go to jail for the very same reason during World War I he was obviously a man of very strong principles.

After leaving the Savoy I regretted not having raised the Eden affair — even though I did keep reminding myself that it was hardly the climate in which to favour the Tories. Mr Eden's honorary Air Commodoreship of 486 Squadron thus remained a closed book, for I never had the opportunity again to discuss the matter with Mr Fraser. He died in 1950 and is best remembered as New Zealand's war-time Prime Minister.

I have often wondered since, whether it was New

The author and Lord Tedder.

Zealand's 1943 general election or Mr Fraser's disenchantment with Mr Eden's involvement in the Balkans débâcle that caused him to turn his back on 486 Squadron's proposal. I have a strong feeling it could have been the former as there is nothing so sharp and cutting as a politician's campaign sword.

Mr Eden was later to become Prime Minister of Great Britain. 486 Squadron too, reached the pinnacle of its profession. By the war's end it had destroyed more than 80 enemy aircraft and 223 flying bombs. It had also acquitted itself well as a low attack fighter bomber force, sinking

Rocket firing Typhoons, Thorney Island May 1944.

several ships and acting as close support to the Allied armies from Normandy to Berlin. Marshal of the RAF, Lord Tedder, paid it the supreme tribute when he said, '486 (NZ) Squadron was the most versatile and possibly the hardest worked squadron in World War II'.

I was to see a good deal of Tedder. As Deputy Supreme Commander to Eisenhower, he became a frequent visitor to 123 Wing during our campaign in Europe. Like many pipe-smokers, he was a deep thinker, and it could be depended upon that the few questions he asked were designed to catch me off balance.

Eisenhower and Leigh-Mallory were completely opposite types. Although we only had the two visits from Eisenhower, I was left with the impression that no general of his time could have filled his shoes. He was a great diplomat, and brilliant co-ordinator. Just to keep Patton and Montgomery from each other's throats must have required a degree of divine power. His firm handshake and broad open smile made me feel I had made a friend for life.

Leigh-Mallory on the other hand was inclined to be dour and was thus not the smiling type, but he was a great champion of his aircrew and consequently a frequent visitor to our Wing. All three were ardent supporters of our rocket-firing Typhoons and much of our success was due to the interest and encouragement shown by these three high level members of Overlord's top brass.


The airborne rocket was a comparatively new addition to the RAF's armoury, yet its basic principle was almost as old as Methuselah. The Chinese had used rocket-propelled arrows against the Mongols nigh on 700 years earlier. Why it hadn't been resurrected to an airborne role by the RAF in the early days of the war is hard to understand. Once taken up by Coastal Command and used against enemy shipping — particularly in the U-boat war — it became the Germans' most feared weapon.

Each Typhoon, when armed with eight rockets and four 20 mm Hispano cannons, packed a power punch equal — if not superior — to the broadside of a medium-sized battle cruiser. An RAF squadron comprised 22 aircraft, 12 on immediate readiness and the balance on routine repair and maintenance. Thus 123 Wing's four squadrons were the equivalent of a sizeable airborne battle fleet. However, it was in support of land forces that the Typhoon reigned supreme. Armed with rockets or bombs and its hard hitting 20 mm cannons, it was to alter the whole concept and calibre of close support operations.

Soon after arriving at Thorney Island, Wing Commander E. P. Brooker, DFC joined us as Wing Commander Flying. Quiet and softly spoken, he had won his spurs during the Battle of Britain before being posted out to the Far East where he had quite a rugged time escaping from the Japanese. If the squadrons took to him slowly, they followed him faithfully and he became a first class and popular leader. Unhappily his stay was all too short. Like many of the boys who hurled themselves at the Atlantic Wall he was shot down by flak and killed.

While most of the 2nd TAF Typhoons were heavily engaged attacking flying bomb sites, 123 Wing was allotted the task of destroying all German radar stations between Cap Gris Nez and the Channel Islands. It was an unenviable task for, from a low attack pilot's point of view, they were without doubt amongst the hardest targets to approach and winkle out. Relatively small, they all held a commanding view and no matter which way you approached them you could never surprise them. It was a cruel period in the history of the Wing and we lost many pilots before we were able to clear the way for D-Day.

Besides Wing Commander Brooker our Wing lost six squadron commanders within a period of three weeks. Attacks on such targets are described in some detail in my book *Typhoon Pilot*, but I think one in particular bears repeating:

> . . .one such attack was by four of our aircraft on the radar station at Cap de La Hague/Joburg on 24 May. This mission was led by Squadron Leader Niblett of 198 Squadron, who was killed a week later when attacking a similar target at Dieppe. His report read: '32 x 60 pound rockets and cannons were fired. One missing aircraft seen to crash at base of installation. Flight Sergeant Vallely crashed on target.'

Group Captain Desmond Scott explains the rocket attachments on a Typhoon to General Eisenhower at Gilze Rijen in November 1944. In the background is Wing Commander W. Dring, who was killed a few weeks later in the Ardennes campaign.

A German soldier who saw this attack and was captured some months later, was so impressed that he insisted on recounting it to his interrogators:

Three Typhoons came in from the valley, flying very low. The second aircraft received a direct hit from 37 mm flak which practically shot off the tail. The pilot, however, managed to keep some sort of control and continued straight at the target. He dived below the level of the radar structure, fired his rockets into it and then tried at the last moment to clear it. The third aircraft, in trying to avoid the damaged Typhoon, touched the latter's fuselage, and both crashed into the installation. This radar site was never again serviceable. Of the cables leading up to the target, 23 out of the 28 major leads were severed.

On the strength of our own evidence, and this German report, I later recommended the young pilot of the damaged Typhoon, Flying Officer Harold Freeman of the Royal Canadian Air Force, for a posthumous Victoria Cross, but to no avail. He had carried out many dangerous operations, and when you appreciate that any one of them could have been a major episode in the life of any soldier or sailor — or many airmen too for that matter — I considered my bitterness over this denial fully justified.

It seemed to be a grave miscarriage of justice, particularly when compared with our Senior Service. After its brief skirmish against the pocket battleship *Graf Spee* at the mouth of the River Plate, the crews of the three British ships involved were awarded no less than 74 decorations for gallantry. These included one knighthood, six DSOs, 17 DSCs and 45 DSMs. In retrospect, however, they may have been well earned, for this brief battle proved conclusively that conventional naval weapons were already outdated. Before scuttling herself for lack of fuel, the *Graf Spee* had to fire off 41 rounds for each hit scored, the *Exeter*, 64 and the *Ajax* and *Achilles*, no less than 121 between them!.

Thus the resurrection of the rocket was not before its time. As confirmed in Coastal Command in the latter years of the war — and more recently in the Falklands — its arrival was to create a new dimension in the affairs of men.

# Fourteen
# The Road To The
# Rhine

Much has been written about the Normandy campaign: D-Day, Overlord, the struggle for Europe. It has been presented by everyone from generals to privates and by post-war historians. It would only be covering much-harrowed ground if I filled these pages with a repetition of the events as I saw them during this, the greatest combined operation of all time. Suffice it to say that we in the RAF, like the other two services, played our part to the best of our ability whether we served in Coastal, Bomber, or Fighter Command, or the 2nd Tactical Air Force. Each played its important part in the Allied victory in Europe.

Coastal Command is well remembered for its performance in the Battle of the Atlantic — a battle that raged for five and a half years, and in the words of the

Crash and burn up. A 115 Squadron Lancaster (KO-G).

Admiralty, 'The most protracted and bitterly fought campaign in which the British Empire and her allies had ever been engaged.'

Bomber Command is best known for its courageous but often crippling night raids upon the great industrial cities of Hitler's Europe, in particular on his factories and those plants committed to the production of fuel oil; and Fighter Command for its victory in the Battle of Britain. The 2nd Tactical Air Force sprang from the days of the Desert Air Force to become the greatest and most potent force in support of ground troops the world has ever seen.

The RAF had grown both in strength and proficiency since the days of Dunkirk. So much so that in the eyes of the German Generals the battle for Normandy was more of an assault from the skies than the conventional form of warfare, in which land forces had hitherto faced each other in a slugging blood bath. The soldier who had to fight his battles without air cover was dead and buried before they began, as witnessed by the following remarks made by General Bayerlein soon after our assault upon the beaches of Normandy.

The planes kept coming over as if on a conveyer belt and the bomb carpets unrolled in great rectangles. My flak had

A mixed bag of Spitfires on the move over Ursel, Belgium, October 1944.

hardly opened its mouth when the batteries received direct hits which knocked out half my guns and silenced the rest. After an hour I had no communications with anybody, even by radio. By noon nothing was visible but dust and smoke. My front lines looked like the face of the moon and at least 70 percent of my troops were out of action — dead, wounded, crazed or numbed. All my forward tanks were knocked out and the roads practically impassable.

Even the great Rommel, master of the blitzkrieg, had to complain to the German Chief of Staff Field Marshal Keitel on D-plus-six, 12 June 1944:

The enemy is strengthening himself visibly on land under very strong aircraft formations. Our operations are rendered extraordinarily difficult and in part impossible to carry out. The enemy has complete command of the air.

The German generals had good reason to complain, but our own successes were not achieved without a great deal of pain. Our rocket-firing Typhoons and Typhoon fighter bombers bore the brunt of the close air support and many of

Wing Commander Dring standing outside operations set up at B7, better known as Martragny.

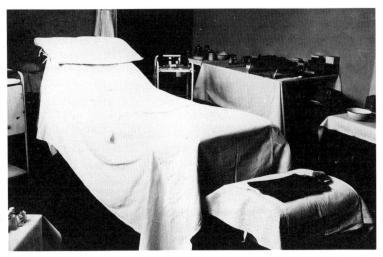

The operating room at Martragny. The author became one of its first patients, when a captured German horse he was riding slipped and rolled on him. Too low to bale out, he broke his leg in three places.

our aircraft were shot down while attacking targets in support of Montgomery's armies.

Most of our losses were from light flak, particularly the four-barrelled variety which hose-piped the sky with its murderous tracer. When hit, most pilots were too low to bale out and crashed their burning Typhoons into the ground without so much as a whisper.

One tragic case was a little Canadian. He was hit in the spine and paralysed from the waist down. His aircraft did not catch fire and he was still able to switch on his transmitter and give us a calm commentary on his predicament. He was even able to keep his Typhoon in horizontal flight, but the injuries he sustained soon took control and with a sad message of farewell he went into a shallow dive, hit the ground and exploded into a great ball of fire.

For all who served in 2nd TAF the invasion of Normandy would have been the busiest time of their lives. As airfield commander of 123 Wing I would often stand alongside our Martragny strip near Bayeux and watch aircraft from my four squadrons scrambling through great clouds of dust as they took off or landed in a never-ending procession. Above all this was the noise of the German gunfire from across the

River Orne. It sounded like an orchestra of drums, a loud bashing and crashing that reached a crescendo in the Battle for the Falaise Gap.

I was a frequent visitor to the front line during our time in Normandy. These visits gave me the opportunity to see at first hand the value of our air-to-ground co-operation. We had trained Air Force observers riding around in tanks and armoured cars in the forward areas. These officers were in radio contact with our cab-rank of Typhoons patrolling overhead. Working on the same grid system they would guide our aircraft onto targets such as tanks, troop concentrations, mobile field guns and mortar positions. Our combined efforts were as near to perfection as they would ever be. However, sometimes our ground controllers would lose their vehicles through enemy action and contact would be lost. But the Army would generally find a quick solution by firing off coloured markers. Anything beyond the perimeter of this line was fair game and our Typhoons would sweep in low on anything that moved. They could outgun the dreaded enemy 88s and explode the heaviest tanks. German road convoys were quite a different matter. Like our attacks from Tangmere on the E-boat flotillas in the previous year, it was every man for himself, and the carnage and destruction our Typhoons meted out to those who were cluttering up the roads was fearsome to behold. The battle for the Falaise Gap was a typical example of tactical air power at its most productive. The enemy, realising it was being surrounded by a steel net, took to the roads in thousands, and the highways and byways in the area of Falaise became a bloodbath of monstrous proportions.

General Bayerlein, who had also been caught up in this hell from the skies, later described it as follows:

Typhoons swept in low over at least 250 of my motor transport, trucks, cannon and Nebelwerfer, on the roads in and around the village, and in nearby fields and orchards. They hit a truck train of rocket ammunition right off the bat, and this started exploding and throwing rockets in all directions. The streets were so littered with burning autos, trucks and other equipment, they became impassable.

This interrogation concerns 13 August and was only a prelude to what was to follow during the days leading up to 30 August when we began crossing the Seine.

One afternoon soon after the Falaise Gap had been closed, I took several of my pilots to the area to let them see the results of their efforts. It was a sight that is hard to describe. Shattered tanks and trucks. Tangled masses of both men and horses. Some men caught up and roasted in the blackened hedgerows. The roads and byways around Falaise were a tragic and horrifying sight, but it was the fate of the horses that upset me most. It was not their war. Nor could they reason why. Harnessed as they were, they had no chance to escape. For centuries this noble beast had been man's companion and loyal servant, ploughed his fields and lightened his burdens in many different ways. As they lay dead in tangled heaps, their large wide eyes seemed to cry out to me in anguish. It was a sight that wrenched at the soul. A sight that even after all these years still disturbs my dreams.

Another time when I was up in the forward area near Caen, I came upon a family of white shell-shocked ducks on the side of the road. There would have been about two dozen of them, huddled together and so stunned they were quite oblivious of what was happening around them. An

On the way through Caen with a reconnaissance party to look at a new airstrip near Le Tréport (B35).

army corporal began putting them out of their misery and throwing them into the back of my jeep. I was about to thank him for his generosity when four Typhoons screamed overhead and fired their rockets at a target some distance ahead of us. As they flew into a hail of flak, one caught fire, pulled up into a vertical climb and exploded. The corporal looked at me, and with wide eyes said, 'Cor blimey Sir, I wouldn't 'ave your job for quids.' 'No Corporal,' I replied, 'and I wouldn't have yours either.'

With that all hell broke loose as German shells began bursting all around us. We both dived into the same slit trench and landed on top of two dead Germans — blonde-haired youngsters who were obviously members of the Hitler Youth Brigade. It was rather cramped and we spent a few uncomfortable minutes in this grave-like hole before the barrage lifted and I was able to scramble out and sprint for my jeep.

Our victory at Falaise was the beginning of the end of Hitler's tenure of Normandy and our armies were soon in hot pursuit as the remnants of his 7th Army fled across the Seine.

'In the Ops Caravan' (at B7, Normandy), by William Dring, official war artist.

123 Wing took every opportunity to keep up with the advance and moved rapidly towards the Pas de Calais by way of airstrips near Deauville (B23) and Le Tréport (B35). With Le Havre, Boulogne, Calais and Dunkirk by-passed by our land forces, 123 Wing's commitments became even more widely dispersed, for we now had to look backwards as well as forwards while keeping up with the tempo of Montgomery's drive towards the Rhine. Sometimes our Typhoons would be operating over all four ports at the same time.

The enemy troops locked up in these channel ports still fought back like wounded tigers and shot down many pilots of my Wing. Although Antwerp was captured intact, much blood was to flow before we could use it as a port.

I could never understand why Montgomery called on Bomber Command to add to the weight of our own operations. While we advanced from Normandy to the Rhine in the space of four weeks, 28 000 tons of bombs were dropped on the besieged ports. Eight thousand tons on Le Havre on 11 September when Antwerp, 250 miles nearer the battlefront, had already been captured a week before!

Montgomery's tactics did not come within my compass, but I couldn't help feeling his demands upon Bomber Command were a serious misuse of air power. Bomber

Dispatch riders, 123 Wing.

Command was a strategic weapon of great importance and it should never have been diverted from its primary role of stabbing deep into the heart of Germany, attacking her synthetic oil plants and focal areas of communication.

# Fifteen
# Victory In Europe

We had just flown the squadrons into Merville, a permanent airfield near Lille, when one of our Typhoons overshot the runway and ended upside down in the mud. All who witnessed this incident rushed over to the aircraft in the hope of rescuing its stricken pilot. The surrounding ground was too soft to support the mobile crane and there was little hope of lifting the seven ton aircraft by hand — try as we did. Some Spitfire pilots from 135 Wing which occupied the other side of the airfield from our own joined us, but it was a forlorn effort and the unfortunate pilot was literally drowned in his cockpit. The heavy flak losses my squadrons had suffered were hard enough to bear, but to lose a boy in the Merville mud seemed totally unfair.

I was sadly surveying the scene and thinking how cruel and unforgiving a Typhoon could be, when I felt a hand on my shoulder. It was Chalky White. The same hand that had almost put me through the ceiling two years earlier at Westhampnett. He hadn't changed. A little older perhaps. All he said was 'What a hell of a way to die.' The boy was barely 19 and had only recently joined my Wing. We squelched back onto the concrete perimeter track where I had left my stationwagon. Chalky had a vehicle there too, a captured Citroen. I didn't ask him how he had acquired it as most of my pilots had captured cars too, but I noticed when he proudly showed me his prize that it still had dried blood on the front seat and there were several bullet holes in a door.

After asking him about the fortunes of some of the 485 Squadron boys, I reminded him of our last meeting and our bus ride from Kings Lynn to Sutton Bridge. He said he faintly recalled it. I thought, 'What a man! Who could ever forget a scene like that?' He casually told me a lot had happened since then. He had been shot down near Le Havre in the summer of 1943 and had managed to make his way back to England via Spain and without the help of the Underground movement. Even his gravelly voice couldn't disguise his pleasure at that. Without the help of the Underground! It was the equivalent of climbing Mt Everest without oxygen. I didn't tell him that I had learned from Intelligence much of his escape story and asked him if he would like to bring one of his fellow New Zealanders over to my caravan that evening for a drink. He arrived with a Taihape boy, Frank Transom, and after a whisky or two, Chalky began relating the story of his incredible escape.

After being shot down by a bunch of FW-190s he had avoided his German pursuers by hiding in a water barrel that stood alongside a château on the outskirts of Le Havre. When darkness fell he set off on a journey that was to cover almost 2000 miles. Firstly to Paris where he found temporary refuge in a Montmartre brothel. Through occupied France where he was forced to put a revolver bullet through a German guard who was unlucky enough to question his identity. Vichy France and over the Pyrenees and into Spain, to Barcelona and Madrid. It was a long and hazardous journey, yet he considered his greatest enemies had been his ingrown toenails and the staff at the British Consulate in Barcelona. The latter had apparently regarded his escape story as too incredible and he was suspected of being a German agent. Finally cleared of this, he was put aboard a four-engined Liberator bomber at Gibraltar, but before it started up to fly to England he was off-loaded to make way for a senior army officer. The aircraft lifted from the runway, climbed away towards England, turned on its back and crashed into the sea. There were no survivors.

It was late by the time Chalky had finished his story and after my guests had departed I flopped onto my stretcher and began reliving Chalky's escape and thinking of the long term effects such an experience could have on him. How was the world going to treat men of his calibre when the war was over. In comparison with the Continent, New Zealand was an island in the sun — so far removed from Hitler's war-torn Europe that people who were not involved would never understand. Those pilots who survived the flak storms would be strangers in their own land, disillusioned and bewildered. It had happened after the first war. It could happen again.

I dozed off to the sound of heavy bombers — 1576 aircraft from Bomber Command — carrying a record 5453 tons of bombs, on their way to Duisburg.

A few days later I left Merville and took my squadrons into Ursel — a Belgian airfield midway between Eecloo and Bruges, which had been used by the Italians during the Battle of Britain. It only had the one runway and was barely large enough to accommodate my own four squadrons, so the Spitfires of 135 Wing which included 485 (NZ) Squadron were unable to follow us.

Arnhem, or 'Market Garden' as it was called, became the next major battleground in our assault upon Europe. It is a battle that will be argued about for generations to come. I can only speak as an airman, but having been in close support of Montgomery's armies with my 123 Wing throughout the blistering days of Normandy and the subsequent race for the Rhine, I am still at a loss to understand why the Arnhem airborne landings should have taken precedence over the clearing of the Scheldt. Our race for the Rhine had stretched our supply lines to the limit and the port of Antwerp had become a major factor in the success or failure of our advance on the Ruhr.

These hangars at Ursel had been used by the Italians in 1940.

It almost appeared as though Montgomery was trying to emulate the deeds of the American General George Patton, whose rapid advance against a lightly held right flank bore no comparison with operations on the left. If this was the case he chose the wrong time of year. Whereas the RAF had acknowledged (after painful experience) the effect autumn could have on the face of Holland — or indeed on the whole of western Europe — Montgomery appeared to be too steeped in the conditions of his desert campaigns, where the sun normally smiled and operations could be planned without paying too much attention to the vagaries of the weather. Had the aircraft of 2nd TAF been allowed fully into the picture, there was a slim chance that Market Garden might have borne a little fruit; but the seed bed was already covered in poison ivy, and worse, the harvest season had already gone.

After our defeat in Arnhem we were still faced with the vital need to clear the Scheldt. Antwerp was some 70 miles inland from the sea and it appeared as if Montgomery's eyes had been so firmly fixed on the Ruhr that he grossly underestimated the value of attacking the islands of the Scheldt so that entry to Antwerp could be a foregone conclusion. This meant clearing out the Breskens pocket on

Typhoons taking off from Ursel.

the west side of the Scheldt and the island of Walcheren on the other. To help him achieve this he again asked for Bomber Command's support, and using the heaviest of bombs, the dykes on Walcheren near Westkapelle were breached and 25 square miles of the island flooded. It was a painful decision as far as the Dutch inhabitants were concerned, but the higher perimeter of the island was well fortified by heavy naval guns set deep in steel and concrete installations. So important did the need for Antwerp become, Eisenhower insisted that no further delay would be countenanced and the battle for the Scheldt Estuary must begin no later than 1 November. As in Arnhem, the weather was again the most important factor. Although the Canadians under General Simonds had brought great pressure on the Breskens pocket, the weather prevented Bomber Command from softening up those areas on

One of the author's pilots building a snow replica of his New Zealand Group Captain. Ardennes, January 1945.

The RAF bombing Gilze Rijen airfield, before 123 Wing moved in. The photograph was taken by a young Dutch civilian boy.

Walcheren that were offering the stiffest resistance.

The Canadians, after attacking under appalling conditions, finally captured the town of Breskens on 22 October and the all-out assault on Walcheren began as scheduled, on 1 November. Again the weather was atrocious, and the battleships supporting the landing craft, the *Warspite* and her two monitors, were faced with the added problem of having their spotter aircraft fog-bound in England. Likewise all 2nd TAF airfields were unoperational, except our own airstrip at Ursel, and it too was less than marginal.

The squadrons took off at some risk and I was most thankful to find that the nearer we approached the target area — the stretch of coast between Flushing and Westkapelle — the more friendly became the weather. In fact by the time we were in position, the ceiling had lifted to 500 feet and the forward visibility to several miles.

The German coastal batteries had already created havoc among the attacking Allied landing craft. Out of 25 such vessels mounting rockets and light artillery that attacked the island fortifications near Westkapelle, nine had been sunk and 11 more put out of action.

It is unfortunate that the weather prevented us from arriving earlier, for once on the scene, our rocket-firing

A crashed Typhoon which just missed the author's caravan. Gilze Rijen, November 1940.

Typhoons wasted no time in blasting into the heavy German coastal guns that were causing all the trouble. Our airborne rockets began flying thick and fast as the four squadrons raked the island's coast from Westkapelle to Flushing. While our Typhoons engaged the enemy, commando troops of the 4th Special Service Brigade took advantage of the diversion and landed near the gap made by Bomber Command on 5 October. Some even sailed straight through the gap and attacked the German defences from the rear. To confirm our own views we received that night a signal from Admiral Ramsay, the Allied Naval Commander-in-Chief of Europe:

> The timely and well executed support by your rocket-firing Typhoons when 80 percent of the landing craft were out of action undoubtedly was a vital factor in turning the scales to our advantage.

Ursel had served its purpose well, but I didn't like its poor surface and cramped dispersal areas, and was more than pleased when we vacated it and moved to Gilze Rijen, a permanent Dutch airfield halfway between Breda and Tilburg.

A hundred minesweepers were rushed into the Scheldt to clear the way, and the port of Antwerp was ready to receive

The beginning of an unequal battle against the snow in the Ardennes.

shipping on 28 November — almost a month after the fall of Walcheren.

It was just as well there had been no further delays, for contrary to Montgomery's prediction that the war would be over by Christmas, our supply position had become almost critical and there was still no sign of victory. The Germans were already well aware of our predicament, for they had begun mobilising for a full blast desperate bid to re-capture Antwerp. It was a black and anxious Christmas for the Allies.

The Luftwaffe began receiving its revolutionary jet aircraft in ever increasing numbers. The German navy was also in for a new lease of life through the arrival of a vastly superior type of submarine. Flying bombs continued to create havoc in Brussels and Antwerp, while huge rockets from across the Maas in occupied Holland still rained down on the long suffering Londoners. Field Marshal von Rundstedt's forces, including several Panzer Divisions, burst through the Ardennes and created a great deal of alarm and despondency in the Allied camp.

The snow in the Ardennes favoured the Germans, for they were well versed in those conditions through their experiences on the Russian front. It was a bold gamble on Hitler's part nevertheless, but the Allies' heavy bombers had already beaten him to the punch. No modern army can exist

An example of the damage that was sustained by our aircraft.

— let alone fight — when it is starved of its fuel supplies. By flattening the enemy's synthetic oil plants, the 8th American Air Force and Bomber Harris's heavyweights had forced the Wehrmacht onto its knees. The Luftwaffe was often grounded and whole Panzer Divisions became stranded in the mire. For the Germans, the Blitzkrieg had suddenly become a thing of the past.

The enemy still held all the territory north and east of the Rhine, but their withdrawal from the Ardennes spelt the beginning of the end. As a parting gesture, the Luftwaffe, which had fought so gallantly on all fronts, scraped together enough fuel for a last stab at those airfields inhabited by the 2nd TAF. Close on 1000 fighters — mostly ME-109s and FW-190s — were let loose in low-level attacks against the RAF, creating a great deal of chaos and grievously wounding themselves in the process. Nearly 300 Allied aircraft were set on fire or badly damaged. The Luftwaffe lost nearly 200, many piloted by their most experienced leaders.

123 Wing had moved from Gilze Rijen to the Ardennes at this time and thus missed the attention of the Luftwaffe, but that night — 1 January 1945 — we could hear their bombers looking for us. They sounded like JU88s, but visibility was so poor they were unable to find our snowbound airfield. It was like playing a dangerous game of hide and seek. I could even

A Flying Fortress, crashed at Ursel.

picture the crews huddled in their cockpits, eyes staring at their instruments or giving a quick glance into the blackness below. Young men in their late teens or early twenties. All balancing on that invisible line that every aircrew member follows between life and death.

With the Russians putting mounting pressure on the eastern front, the Allies' next objective was to cross the Rhine. By this time (24 March), they had fully recovered from the Ardennes reverses, were re-grouped, well supplied and ready for action. Led by thousands of aircraft, many towing gliders, others carrying paratroopers, they moved into the area of land between Emmerich and Wesel, on the north side of the Rhine — the first stepping-stone in the advance into Germany. The enemy did not give in easily. Their troops fought ferociously with a fanaticism born of desperation, but the great weight of the Russian advance in the east, and our own efforts in the west, were too much to counter, and Berlin was captured by the red tide on 2 May 1945. The war against Germany finally came to an end on 7 May when a document of unconditional surrender was signed by Germany, the Western Allies and the Russians. So ended the struggle for Europe. It was the end of the bitterest and bloodiest war in the history of mankind.

From the Allies' point of view the conquest of the air was

the predominant factor in winning the war against Germany. Yet it had been the Germans themselves who had set the pattern and shown us the way. The bombing of Warsaw, Belgrade, Rotterdam and Coventry, and the Wehrmacht's speedy advance through Europe under cover of her blitzkrieg were painful early lessons that we had not ignored. In building up our Air Force and concentrating our efforts against Germany, Bomber Command alone became as much the saviour of England as the pilots who fought in the Battle of Britain.

It had been the RAF which had taken the fight to Germany after the Allied Armies had been banished from the Continent — the only offensive within the Allies' power. It was the RAF which had caused the Germans to employ over two million troops on anti-aircraft defence on the Western Front, troops that could well have been employed against the Russians, or in Rommel's Desert Campaign.

As the war progressed and we were joined by the Flying Fortresses of the 8th American Air Force, we had been able to expand our activities and broaden our horizons. With the heavyweights of Bomber Command covering the German cities by night, and the 8th Air Force Flying Fortresses attacking them by day, Germany had felt the product of her own invention — the holocaust of Hamburg, Cologne, Dresden and Berlin. As Germany was flattened city by city, the Luftwaffe found it necessary to withdraw much of its strength from the Russian front. Not only aircraft, but thousands upon thousands of anti-aircraft guns — mainly the dreaded 88 mm, a dual purpose weapon which could have had a profound influence upon Germany's fortunes on her Eastern front.

While Bomber Command had hammered away at the heart of Germany, Coastal Command fought a desperate war against the U-boat packs that had patrolled the sea lanes far beyond England's shores.

Throughout the war the German U-boats had sunk more than 2500 merchant ships of a total of some 14 million tons. During this battle between sea and sky Germany had lost 730 submarines. Nearly 300 of these had been the victims of Coastal Command. A further 47 had been sunk by naval craft operating together with the RAF.

Bomber Command destroyed 80 U-boats during strategic attacks on Germany's own ports or in mine-laying operations along the enemy coast. Rocket-firing Typhoons, whose activities were normally confined to close support of our Armies, had sunk eight U-boats while operating from German bases towards the end of the war.

The Allied Armies had also received strong support from the RAF. The birth of the 2nd Tactical Air Force had seen to this. It was our answer to the blitzkrieg, on a much greater and more professional scale. As our armies had approached the beaches of Normandy to begin their crusade through Europe, the skies became filled with the greatest force of close support aircraft the world had ever seen. Fighter bombers and rocket-firing Typhoons were to blast a pathway from the beaches of Normandy to the waters of the Rhine.

None of this had been achieved without a great deal of pain. The RAF lost over 70 000 highly trained aircrew — 47 000 from Bomber Command alone. A generation of young men no nation could afford to lose.

# Sixteen
# The Day Of Reckoning

The day Germany capitulated, I was mapping out a course to fly from Nijmegen to Dunkirk, when there was a loud thump on the door of my caravan. It was Chalky White, accompanied by none other than my pheasant shooter friend, Flight Lieutenant Lyndon P. Griffiths. I was so pleased to see they had both survived, and after a drink to celebrate our good fortune asked them if they would like to come with me to Dunkirk. I had lost several pilots over the port and was hoping some had survived the flak and become prisoners, or at worst, hospital patients. Neither Chalky nor Griff needed a second invitation and we set off next morning in an Anson aircraft for Mardyke airfield near Dunkirk.

While piloting this twin-engined aircraft I asked Griff if he would be kind enough to roll me a cigarette. I was half way through smoking this when it exploded in my face. Griff, while rolling it, had included a few match heads. It gave me

Nijmegen, Holland.

quite a start but I tried my best not to appear surprised. When I finally looked around into the body of the aircraft some five minutes later, Griff was sitting back in his seat peeling a hard-boiled egg and with a triumphant grin on his face.

Most of the country around the port of Dunkirk had been flooded, and any escape routes the Germans might try to use were well covered by a brigade of Czechs. Although Germany had surrendered on 7 May, Dunkirk for some reason, held out for another day. We didn't know this until we were met at Mardyke airfield by a Czech lieutenant colonel. However, he was just as eager to enter the port as we were, and after obtaining the necessary passes from his HQ to allow us through the road block, we set off in a jeep down a long straight road that led to the town. We hadn't gone far when we saw a bunch of civilians gathered around what appeared to be a blacksmith's forge. I was concerned that the road into Dunkirk might be mined and asked the Czech lieutenant colonel, who spoke passable French, to tell this idle band to walk ahead until we could gather up enough Germans to take their place.

We had only travelled about half a mile when we came upon several Germans standing around the rubble of a partly bombed out building. Most stood and stared, others scowled, but as far as we could see none carried arms. One young member of the Wehrmacht walked towards us with his hands in the air and smiling nervously, welcomed us to Dunkirk — in almost perfect English. On questioning him we learnt that he had attended school in England, and that as far as he knew, we were the first of the Allies to re-enter the port of Dunkirk. He said the road ahead was safe, but we took no chances and made him lead the way along with a squad of his fellow countrymen. Once in the town centre, I dismissed our advance guard, but retained the services of the young interpreter. He had been a lucky find. In conducting us on a tour of the town he directed us to everything he thought would be of interest, and explained in detail whatever we asked of him. Dunkirk was a shambles. The tremendous pounding it had taken from Bomber Command and the 2nd Tactical Air Force was absolutely devastating. Huge areas resembled the surface of the moon, yet the 14 000 Germans trapped in the town when the Allied Armies had by-passed them, had adapted themselves to an eight-month siege in true teutonic fashion. Like badgers, they had gone to earth. Their underground quarters, panelled in varnished timbers, had built-in bunks and wardrobes, and the floors were well carpeted. Most of these underground rooms were better furnished than our RAF stations back in England.

Also stabled underground were several herds of milk cows. These animals were driven to the surface at night to graze through the town where grass grew thickly on the roadsides, and in areas flattened by much earlier bombings. All the cows were in splendid condition and had obviously been well cared for. The German troops too, were a credit to their units. Although many wore faded uniforms, these were all clean and in good repair, and their occupants carried themselves as do all well-disciplined troops. Most looked tired and few showed any desire to be friendly; nor did they display any animosity towards us, except when we were about to enter the hospital. A young Wehrmacht doctor, impeccably dressed, made it quite plain that the hospital was much cleaner without our presence. His four visitors were all armed with .38 calibre Smith and Wessons and with the help of our young interpreter we were able to make him listen to reason. Unfortunately the hospital contained no British air crew, but we found many graves in the military cemetery. Some were occupied by pilots from my own Wing. All had the same simple white wooden cross. All bore the same poignant inscription — 'He died for England.'

The German admiral in charge of the port was still in residence but would only be seen by an officer of equivalent rank or higher. However, I wasn't disappointed in that, for it was the Czech brigade which kept him there and thus its commander's privilege to escort him out.

It was a most interesting day and by the time we had landed back at Nijmegen we were each possessed of a much greater respect for and understanding of our former adversaries. Regrettably this was to be badly tarnished a few days later. I was invited by a staff officer from General Crerar's First Canadian Army to visit Belsen concentration camp and the prison at Celle where the Belsen guards had been detained.

Since Chalky and Griffiths had acted as worthy lieutenants on the trip into Dunkirk, I again invited them to accompany me. Belsen was indescribable. Never before in the long history of the human race could man's inhumanity towards his own kind have sunk to such depths. The dead and the dying. The stench and the pitiful pleadings. The large eyes that cried out from silent faces. We didn't stay long, for it was a most shattering and soul-searing experience.

In the afternoon we visited Celle jail and met many of the culprits. The first cell we were shown contained the bitch of Belsen — Irma Gries. She sat on her bunk and scowled at us like a trapped tiger. In the next cell was a large fat middle-aged blonde with her hair scraped up in a tight bun. On entering her cell, she screamed at one of her jailers and received a powerful backhander across the face. As we moved on to the next cell, even Griff's face had lost some of its colour. Many of the less important guards were crowded into cells, so many in fact that they had to take turns at lying down, and as the doors were opened the air hit us in the face like the blast from a stinking laundry.

Most of the inmates looked extremely ill. In one such cell, a German soldier lay on the floor and when he didn't rise to the command of our interpreter — a large Dutch woman — she moved in quickly and sunk a heavy hob-nailed boot into his ribs. There was a sickening crunch, and I'm sure it must have killed him, for there was no other sound except for murmurs of protest from the other inmates. These were quickly silenced and the cell door slammed and locked.

By this time I had seen enough and I think both Chalky and Griff were also thankful when I asked our Canadian hosts to lead us outside. We were taken into a large brick courtyard that appeared to be the centre of the Celle prison complex. Fifty or sixty German guards were being put through their paces by a short, thickset sergeant-major. He must have been an ex-boxer, as his nose was spread across his face and he had two cauliflower ears.

It was a relief to be out in the open again, but such relief was short-lived. While walking down a line-up of German prisoners the sergeant-major suddenly stopped, and swinging a fist from almost ground level, crashed it into the face of one of his captives. The Belsen jailer would have been unconscious before he hit the ground, and was hurriedly pulled away by the legs as if he were a sack of potatoes.

The Belsen jailers had been brought to book, but the brutality so blatantly displayed by both victors and vanquished was horrific, and I was greatly relieved when we were escorted to the main gates. The normally irrepressible Chalky and Griff sat in stunned silence as we drove off through the battered town and into the bomb-scarred countryside of a defeated Germany.

# *Epilogue*

As I read through this brief script of the war as I saw it I am reminded of its tragedies and of the good fortune many of us experienced in escaping its reaper. I am also driven to ponder some of the larger, unanswered questions of the war.

What would have happened in the Battle of Britain had Hitler insisted that Göring keep forcing his Luftwaffe on England's hard pressed airfields and the factories that gave birth to their tenants? Why did he turn on Russia when he could have directed his energies and his huge resources in an all-out drive for Suez?

Journey's end: this shot was taken in Copenhagen soon after VE Day.

What kind of a man would turn his back on the jet when he could so easily have caught us flat-footed? Or held his night fighter force away from the cramped and over-crowded British bomber bases — a mistake that caused so much pain to his cites and, in the final analysis, dragged him to defeat?

However, we must be thankful for all that had gone before. As the war in Europe drew to a close, we had already entered the shadow of the Atom. It burst above the Japanese city of Hiroshima on the morning of 6 August 1945. It was an event that shattered the world.

Nine months later, as a member of Transport Command, I had occasion to visit Japan. It was a visit that may well have changed my direction. Dresden, Hamburg, Stuttgart, Berlin — none could be compared with this. Only Sir Winston Churchill could have given voice to my feelings as I stood alone in the centre of the wasteland of Hiroshima: 'What ought we to do? Which way shall we turn to save our lives and the future of the world? It does not matter so much to old people; they are going soon anyway, but I find it poignant to look at youth in all its activity and ardour and wonder what would lie before them if God wearied of mankind. . .' But perhaps all this that I fear is mere melancholy and dismay and will fly away as the autumn leaves if I stand again by the old dispersal hut at Tangmere, Manston or Gilze Rijen and listen back through the wartime years. It cannot be that the spirit which once set our young blood afire has left our race forever. Nor could it have been subdued or cast forever in the nightmare of our dreams.

Here the autumn falls upon our River Avon, and near the bend, the tall trees of evening stand golden to the skies. Beneath the sycamores, the shadows deepen, and I am lulled into a sadness by the whispering of the leaves. It's a soft warm breeze that drifts down from the hills filling the world with pine forests, log fires and days of long ago. If only Smithy were here, Spike Umbers, Wally, Steve and Fitz. Just for one more day. Just for one more hour.

Perhaps if I close my eyes we might fly off again to those sunlit uplands where the clouds are full of laughter. Where good fellowship among all men is a never-ending thing.

'Avonlea',
Christchurch
New Zealand